"Rebecca has the unique [...]
as teacher, advocate, and p [...]
sensible examples to assist educators and parents alike.
Students with executive functioning challenges are usually
exasperating to understand and help. This book breaks down
the common roadblocks to organization; offers respectful
observations as to why the student struggles; and ultimately
offers multiple ideas of compassionate alternatives to help the
student attain success."

—*Mary Limbacher, Founder and Executive Director,*
Parents in Toto Autism Resource Center

"*Executive Function "Dysfunction"* is packed with real-world
examples of executive functioning deficits and multiple
strategies to overcome them. A must-read book for all
educators (and parents) who work with students with
organizational, attention, and theory of mind difficulties.
This book is straight-forward, easy to read, and loaded with
specific, relevant strategies that can be used immediately in
the classroom or at home."

—*Lisabeth Watson, Founder and Chief*
Executive Officer, AEP Connections

"An extremely valuable and user-friendly guide for parents
and teachers to understand, educate, and best support children
with executive function impairments. Rebecca Moyes shares
her considerable knowledge and experience in helping
students with disabilities to achieve school success. This book
clearly describes and illustrates the challenges of executive
dysfunction, as well as providing effective strategies, lesson
plans, and expert advice."

—*Sandra F. Rief, M.A., author of* How to Reach and Teach
Children with ADD/ADHD *and* The ADD/ADHD
Checklist: A Practical Reference for Parents and Teachers

Executive Function "Dysfunction"—Strategies for Educators and Parents

by the same author

**Addressing the Challenging Behavior of Children
with High-Functioning Autism/Asperger
Syndrome in the Classroom**
A Guide for Teachers and Parents
Rebecca A. Moyes
ISBN 978 1 84310 719 4
eISBN 978 1 84642 346 8

Incorporating Social Goals in the Classroom
**A Guide for Teachers and Parents of Children with
High-Functioning Autism and Asperger Syndrome**
Rebecca A. Moyes
Foreword by Susan J. Moreno
ISBN 978 1 85302 967 7
eISBN 978 1 84642 194 5

of related interest

**Helping Students Take Control
of Everyday Executive Functions**
The Attention Fix
Paula Moraine
ISBN 978 1 84905 884 1
eISBN 978 0 85700 576 2

Executive Function "Dysfunction"— Strategies for Educators and Parents

Rebecca A. Moyes, M.Ed.

Jessica Kingsley *Publishers*
London and Philadelphia

First published in 2014
by Jessica Kingsley Publishers
73 Collier Street
London N1 9BE, UK
and
400 Market Street, Suite 400
Philadelphia, PA 19106, USA

www.jkp.com

Library of Congress Cataloging in Publication Data
A CIP catalog record for this book is available from the Library of Congress

British Library Cataloguing in Publication Data
A CIP catalogue record for this book is available from the British Library

ISBN 978 1 84905 753 0
eISBN 978 1 78450 045 0

Printed and bound in Great Britain

I dedicate this book to five extra special children that I have had the privilege to know and work with:

For Aaron, a pretty cool artistic kid with a sensitive heart.

For Lexi, a talented, super-kind sibling.

For Benjamin, the cutest three-year-old ever.

For Dylan, a young adult I've grown to truly respect.

And for Sam, a hard-working and compassionate teenager.

For Aaron's, Lexi's, Benjamin, Dylan's, and Dylan's parents: most parents have the love, but you have both the love and the fortitude to champion for what your children need and to empower them to grow and expand their horizons in wonderful ways. Some parents would have given up when presented with the trials that have come your way, but these same challenges have made you stronger. You have truly inspired me. May God bless you and your families and provide you with the courage to continue to be a voice for your kids and for others yet to come.

And lastly, for Mary Limbacher, Lisabeth Watson, and Sandra Rief: a heartfelt thank you for all the work you do on behalf of our special children and for offering your support for the publication of this book.

Contents

CHAPTER ONE

When Interventions Don't Work

Some time ago, I attended a school meeting where a student's parents were asking for support to improve their son's organizational and study skills.

"David never brings home the right materials. We are always making trips back to the school to get his textbooks," explained Mom. "We want you to pack his book bag for him."

"Sometimes he writes his assignments down in the planner, and other times he doesn't. Usually, what he writes is not complete," described Dad. "He needs someone else to write his homework down for him."

"This doesn't just impact at school. If I tell him to go upstairs and do three things; invariably, he only does one or two. He needs multiple prompts to remember things," continued Mom.

"Yes," added Dad. "When we work with him to do his homework, he can't even get his thoughts organized to get started. It takes us three times as long to do the homework than it should normally take. It may seem to you that we don't study for tests. We spend *hours* memorizing definitions or working through problems. There are times we feel that he has learned the material very well, but then he brings home his tests and the score makes you think that he never even looked at the material!"

"Does David work with you in a quiet place, or is the TV or radio on when you're working? I find that many children need a quieter place to learn," his teacher offered.

"No. Homework time is strictly homework time," explained Dad. "What's strange is sometimes he is *over-focused* on one of his special interests—lately it's carpenter ants—and you can't seem to drag him away from it no matter what you do. He has this amazing memory for some things and not others."

"He also seems to have trouble with impulsivity. He doesn't think before he speaks or before he acts. This always gets him into trouble with the kids in his class and with his teachers. If you ask him why he did it when he knows better, he can't give you an answer. He always seems genuinely sorry," his mom said sadly. "Sometimes he's harder on himself than we are."

"Yes, I've seen some of that in my class, too," his teacher agreed softly.

"And he's always losing things. I think we have replaced his glasses at least three times this school year," his dad added. "We usually buy two coats and two hats because we know David will lose one of them."

"Have you tried consequences?" asked the teacher. "Can you take something away that he likes?"

"It's not that he is being disrespectful by not being able to do these things," explained Mom, her voice rising in frustration, "He just can't seem to *remember* or he doesn't *know how* to do these things."

"We feel that he gets plenty of consequences at school. He has lost recess, and he has been put in time-out. All of these things have been used and the only thing that has come out of them is lowered self-esteem," Dad continued. "We are paying for him to see a counselor twice a month because we are concerned about how he feels about himself."

"Well, I think he has the capability to do his own work. I have watched him in class. He's actually a very bright kid," offered the teacher. "He just needs to focus. He's not the worst in my class, I think you should know."

"I agree with that," added the school psychologist, "We have to teach him to be more independent. His IQ scores are actually indicating that he is in the high average range. A child with his ability should be able to pack his backpack without assistance."

"I think by asking us to write down his assignments and to make sure his books are packed in his backpack, we would be enabling him," the principal agreed. "Someone is not going to be able to pack his backpack when he gets to middle school."

Sound familiar? This scenario occurs in schools everywhere in the world. Parents want their children to be successful. They want teachers and administrators to assist them in this effort. Teachers and administrators want students to learn to be responsible.

At the center of this scenario, however, is a lack of understanding for *why* certain students have difficulty in planning, organization, and study skills. For some children, it is a genuine behavioral problem. For one reason or another, schoolwork is not the priority in their young lives. But for a sizeable amount of other students, the problem is not behavioral. It is neurological. These students have a true deficit in their cognitive functioning. This deficit arises in the prefrontal lobes of the brain. Research is providing us with cutting-edge information that explains why children like David can be so weak in some areas of cognitive functioning, but strong in other areas. These weak areas, coined by modern researchers as *executive function deficits*, are being closely examined in recent times to determine their impact in cognition and learning. Interventions to support these children, however, are lagging far behind.

For the student in the above scenario, neither party is exhibiting appropriate knowledge of executive functions. Parents cannot insist that teachers and administrators take over the student's daily activities if the student is going to be independent and productive in his school years and beyond. On the flip side, however, teachers and administrators cannot expect students with executive function deficits to be able to perform tasks that exceed their ability levels without strategies that *teach these students how to be independent.* Sadly, many folks feel that IQ tests are a good barometer to determine whether a student can or cannot do particular activities. But, as we will see, they are not always good indicators of executive function proficiency.

This book is about awareness. As more and more children with learning problems are included in regular education classrooms, teachers need the tools to be able to accommodate and support them meaningfully. It is important for educators and administrators to know that medications may help with some of the symptoms of executive function deficits— they may assist a student to focus better, lower the anxiety associated with feelings of deficiency, or help with cognitive rigidity. But, they do not take away the *frontal lobe insufficiency* as a whole. No medication will eliminate every symptom a child with executive function deficits presents. These students will need supports and accommodations if they are to be successful in the classroom.

This book is also about advocacy. Parents and teachers need to stand ready to make suggestions and implement strategies that will assist their children or students to have successful school experiences. They will need up-to-date information and training to make this happen.

Finally, this book is about hope. There are practical ways that these deficits can be addressed in the classroom to provide meaningful benefits for children who struggle with these issues. All of the worksheets and lesson plans included in this book can also be downloaded from www.jkp.com/catalogue/book/9781849057530/resources. Good teachers are already using them and experiencing success! By showcasing some of these interventions I hope to encourage others to use them in order to provide assistance to as many children as possible. These strategies can make the difference between a student that is left to flounder on his or her own, or a student that can achieve independence and experience success in his school years. After all, shouldn't this goal be the common ground for both parents and educators?

CHAPTER TWO

What Are Executive Functions?

When one begins a study of learning disabilities, it's nearly impossible not to be impressed with the complexity of the brain. We marvel at the intricacy of our neural connections. We begin to appreciate both the brain's fragility, as well as its resilience in the presence of environmental or genetic assaults.

Over the years, there has been intense scrutiny among psychologists regarding the nature of executive functions, i.e., what they are, what they do, and how they impact learning. (See the box on pages 23–24 for examples of executive functions.) Executive functions have been defined as those neuropsychological processes that impact in human self-regulation (Barkley 1997). Self-regulation can best be described as the private talk that we use to alter or adjust our behavior. For instance, consider this example:

• •

A teenager knows that if she misses her 10:30 p.m. curfew this Friday, she will not be allowed to go out with her friends next weekend or use her computer to chat with them the entire upcoming week. Since she previously missed her curfew and was punished for this previously, she has knowledge that this will indeed happen. Consequently, she self-regulates her behavior to avoid this mishap by checking her watch and reminding herself to be heading home by 9:45 p.m.

••

Research studies have provided for us a strong indication that executive functions are regulated by the frontal cortex of the brain, and in particular, by the frontal lobes. Thus, children with an executive function disorder are thought to have some dysfunction in this particular region of the brain.

The frontal lobes are the "executives in charge." They can be compared to the heads of our families, the clergy of our churches, or the supervisors at our places of work. Without good leadership, effective operations will be fragmented and inefficient. So it is, too, with our cognitive abilities. It is our highly developed frontal lobe system that has allowed our species to evolve to the extent that it has. It is the frontal lobes that have enabled some members of our society to become charismatic leaders, gifted musicians and artists, or talented inventors who have devised creative solutions to solve many problems plaguing our civilization (Goldberg 2001). The frontal lobes are necessary for each and every learning experience to be successful.

In contrast, however, frontal lobe damage or dysfunction can wreak havoc in our lives. In older persons, it is the frontal lobes that are affected in individuals diagnosed with Alzheimer's disease or dementia. Memory, attention, and organizational skills are all impacted in this population. But, frontal lobe dysfunction can also be seen in children with learning disability, ADD and ADHD, Tourette's syndrome, schizophrenia, obsessive-compulsive disorder, autism, and Asperger's syndrome. Children with nonverbal learning disorder also typically display frontal lobe dysfunction. These disorders affect a sizeable amount of the student population in any given school today. For this reason, it is important that educators and parents recognize the cognitive deficits associated with frontal lobe dysfunction and create programming to support these children. Consider the following:

••

Mark was a third-grade student in his elementary school. Mark was found to be in the average range of intelligence and carried a diagnosis of Asperger's syndrome. He had tremendous difficulty with social skills—he lacked the ability to perceive what his peers were thinking. If he was being rude or obnoxious, he didn't "read" their signals that he needed to adjust his behavior. Often, Mark was impulsive; but sometimes, he would perseverate on one particular topic of interest in his conversations or play. Mark's teachers were constantly frustrated with his inability to bring homework to and from school, to keep his desk and locker organized, and to begin and follow through with tasks that involved a planning process. Written expression assignments were particularly difficult for him. Mark's teachers felt that if Mark could just "get his act together and try harder" he would be an excellent student, as he certainly had intellectual potential.

••

The above scenario is often a source of frustration for both teachers and parents, not to mention for students who have executive function deficits. These children may experience minimal success academically if they are not found eligible for special education supports. As the gap widens between their performance and the performance of their peers, and particularly in the middle school years when rote teaching gives way to more high-order instruction, these same students may begin to experience the by-products of anxiety and low self-esteem (Holmes 1987).

Students with executive function deficits are often targeted for behavioral consequences when they do not follow through with the expectations of the classroom teacher. In other words, they are judged by school personnel to be noncompliant rather than incompetent. Often what is missing in these classrooms are the accommodations and modifications that would help make the educational experience for such students more successful and would serve to level the playing field for these atypical children.

After a student has qualified for special education classes, his parents may breathe a sigh of relief. They may feel that with the additional help, their child will now begin to make true progress. But this is often the time that parents need to be even more vigilant. Grouping children with special needs together, and adopting a one-size-fits-all program without considering their varied learning needs, can be just as detrimental as placing these students in regular education classes and expecting them to keep up with their peers without the necessary supports:

••

Sarah was a student with nonverbal learning disability. Her performance IQ score was much lower than a verbal IQ score, and she struggled with visual-spacial tasks—she had frequent difficulty with map skills, math computation skills that involved multiple steps, written expression assignments, and social skills. She was eventually placed in a learning support classroom part-time with other children who had learning problems. Sarah did not progress, even in this environment, because much of her new program was not geared to her particular deficits. Sarah used her fingers to count out nearly every math problem. She had reached her peak in being able to complete computations this way. Her writing assignments often appeared "empty"; that is, they had little substance and strayed from the topic. Surprisingly, only one Individualized Education Plan (IEP) goal was written to address all of the above. This goal focused on helping Sarah to function at grade equivalency. The only accommodations provided to her in her regular education classroom were extended timelines for assignments and tests and the ability to take tests in the learning support classroom.

• •

Today, the field of education has readily available a wealth of information regarding special education students and their learning styles or learning preferences. It is important that educators and administrators avail themselves of this research. The more prepared our educators are for the complex needs of children like Sarah and Mark, the better their programs will be. Knowledge of how to support and diagnose children with executive function deficits, however, is still lacking in schools today. School psychologists need to be especially alert so that they can recognize children who present with symptoms of an executive function disorder and be able to select testing instruments that are sensitive to teasing out possible deficits:

• •

Dylan was a student with Tourette's syndrome and ADHD. He began to experience problems in school almost immediately upon entering kindergarten. He could not attend to his teacher. He had difficulty with peers. He was impulsive. Several times he was referred to the special education department for testing by his parents as well as his teachers. The results of Dylan's testing repeatedly found him ineligible for special education services. Dylan's performance IQ was 27 points less than his verbal IQ. The district, when calculating his actual IQ, averaged the two together. This resulting computation was not significantly discrepant from the grades he was receiving in his classroom. Thus, the school district felt that Dylan was not a student of exceptionality, despite his two diagnoses. Only after seeking out the advice and counsel of a neuropsychologist and a special education attorney did Dylan's parents eventually achieve an IEP for their son. Because of special education timelines, however, this IEP was not actually implemented until the end of his fourth-grade year. Dylan, at that time, was already two grade levels behind his peers in several of his subjects. More important was the impact this experience had on his self-esteem. As a fifth-grade student, Dylan was showing symptoms of clinical depression and anxiety.

• •

In the early 1900s, neuropsychologists studied the brains of individuals with lesions to the frontal lobes. It was thought that frontal lobe lesions may be a contributing factor in the problems these individuals were having with regard to attention, memory, and abstract thought, as well as other cognitive functions (Bianchi 1922). Critics of this research, however, compared these studies with those of individuals who had undergone surgery to remove portions of their frontal lobes due to severe epilepsy. These patients, even after surgery, did not suffer a drop in IQ points. The reason for this was not readily evident: frontal lobe insufficiencies are not fully tapped in typical tests of intelligence—those very same tests used in schools today!

We now have knowledge that within the results of cognitive testing completed on children with executive function deficits, there may be clues or footprints in the individual IQ subtests that indicate a need for further evaluation. But skilled evaluators will need to forge additional testing paths to pinpoint them. Unfortunately, these comprehensive evaluations are rarely undertaken in public schools today. Memory skills, social skills, novel problem-solving ability, shifting, and behavioral inhibition may go untapped. And sadly, parents may not know that they need to request such testing for their children. As a result of evaluations that are not sufficient in depth or scope, many children are not qualified for special education services, and they are left to fend for themselves. Worse yet, the child's problems are then labeled as behavioral.

Pennington and Oszonoff (1996) identified four domains of executive functions: inhibition, cognitive flexibility/ shifting, working memory, and planning/initiation. They believed these domains are not discrete; rather, they are interactive and dependent upon each other. The ability to self-monitor and maintain emotional control are also domains that are affected by executive function deficits. As seen previously, individuals with executive function deficits may have difficulty with self-talk—that is, the process of using internal language to monitor behavior. With effective self-talk, along with efficient working memory ability, we can form orderly plans, activate them, and stick to them.

Many children with executive function deficits also have trouble with social skills and theory-of-mind skills. Theory of mind is the ability to know what someone else is thinking. It also includes the ability to know and keep track of what someone else knows about what *we know*. Without theory-of-mind skills, a child's behavior will most likely be coined as socially inappropriate.

All of these executive function deficits will be examined in this book. Although the book consists of individual chapters on various executive functions, it is critical for the reader to understand their interconnectedness. It is extremely difficult to separate each function from the others. For instance, a child who has difficulty with theory-of-mind skills as well as behavioral inhibition problems will experience social difficulties because of both. Even if theory-of-mind skills are addressed, the student may not experience success because of his behavioral inhibition deficits.

Practical strategies for addressing executive function deficits are provided throughout this book. Good teachers are using these strategies in classrooms all over the world and experiencing success. I hope that parents and teachers will be able to modify or adapt these strategies and supports to meet the needs of their individual children/students with executive function deficits.

Examples of Executive Functions

The following is a list of executive functions that may impact on a child's ability to learn:

- Behavioral inhibition: avoiding temptation in actions and words, screening or filtering words and actions to avoid trouble

- Theory of mind: knowing what someone else knows is thinking or feeling

- Working memory: holding necessary information in the forefront so that it can be readily available; accessing recall

- Organizational skills: sequencing, retrieving, establishing and maintaining order

- Initiation: beginning a task or activity

- Motivation: initiating and completing a task or activity

- Planning and time management: analyzing, strategizing, prioritizing, ordering steps to completion

- Attention and filtering: staying with the task until completion, pacing, tuning out distractions

- Self-talk: monitoring, focusing, internal motivation or drive, managing frustration and anger appropriately

- Shifting (transitioning): moving from one task or thinking process to another

- Decision making: adjusting, re-focusing priorities, making choices

- Predicting: understanding consequences to certain behaviors.

CHAPTER THREE
Behavioral Inhibition

Behavioral inhibition is an executive function that develops first, ahead of many other executive functions. Although it is important to understand that the executive functions are interactive (they work together and depend upon each other), it is thought by some researchers that addressing behavioral inhibition will also result in an improvement of the other executive functions in some children (Barkley 1997).

Many children receive consequences for their lack of behavioral inhibition, but this problem behavior may actually be attributed to a *cognitive deficit*. That isn't to say that we should not address in a behavioral fashion problem behaviors that may arise because of this deficit, but we need to be mindful that such children may need to learn by rote the use of behavioral inhibition while other children seem to acquire it in a more natural manner.

We all know children who lack behavioral inhibition; that is, they do not seem to be aware of the social laws that govern behavior and provide for us a framework of appropriateness:

• •

Michael is a seventh-grade student diagnosed with ADHD and Asperger's syndrome. His school-age history is checkered with many incidents of problem behavior. Most of these problems stem from Michael's inability to regulate his actions. His latest stay in the time-out room came about because he took his shirt off in an assembly. When Michael was asked why he did this, he replied, "I was hot." His parents are exasperated with Michael. They claim that he has no inhibition and frequently does not weigh out his actions before initiating them. The school believes that Michael is emotionally disturbed. They believe that he needs a placement in an alternative education program to "straighten him out." Michael's mother described how her son recently took her car keys from the hall table and backed the car out onto the street in front of their house. When she asked him why he did such a thing, he said that he wanted to see what it felt like to drive.

● ●

An inhibition mechanism comes into play when the prefrontal lobes grow and mature. At three or four years of age, preschoolers know what they are supposed to do, and often can tell us; but some of these youngsters may have difficulty inhibiting responses because their inhibition mechanism has not matured. Frequently, parents will catch their preschool child in the act of doing something that is forbidden (e.g. sneaking snack food or manipulating the knobs on an appliance). They will report that even as they are correcting their child, he continues to do the offensive behavior. As children grow and they begin to understand the consequences of their actions, the inhibition component of the executive functions develops. They are then better able to modify their behavior.

One can observe this phenomenon in very young children, who frequently share stories about their families that are personal in nature and may cause their family embarrassment. As the inhibition component matures, these children learn to recognize what thoughts should remain private or how to screen and filter thoughts so that they are more appropriate to say out loud. This inhibition maturity is often-times not evident in children with executive function deficits, and they continue to have difficulty with this skill:

• •

Emily is an eight-year-old girl with Asperger's syndrome. Her parents state that Emily exhibits no filter between what she thinks and what she says. Frequently, Emily will share stories with her teachers and fellow students that cause her family much embarrassment. Recently, she reported to her classmates that her mother had purchased some bra inserts. She announced that her mother was a size 34A and wanted to be a size 36C.

• •

For many individuals with an executive function disorder, it is extremely difficult to learn to monitor their behavior. What seems easy to neurotypical individuals takes much effort and conscious thought for these folks. Loved ones of individuals who have suffered brain damage because of accidents or who are experiencing diseases affecting the brain often report that changes in behavioral inhibition are frequent symptoms or by-products of their accident or illness. Such inhibitions may take the form of overspending, excessive drinking/binging, gambling, or exhibiting risk-type behavior—these may all be symptoms of executive function deficits (i.e. behavioral inhibition) in individuals with brain disease or trauma.

Engaging in risk-type behavior is sometimes seen in children with attention deficit disorder, autism, and Tourette's syndrome. Consider this vignette that was shared by a young adult with Tourette's syndrome:

• •

"When I was in my late teens, I would frequently enjoy touching women's ear lobes. I would often approach women

in the street and be driven by an irresistible urge to caress their ears. Often-times, women would respond with shock. Once, a woman became angry at my behavior and slapped me in the face."
••

An extreme manifestation of executive function deficit with regard to behavioral inhibition can often be found in individuals with Tourette's syndrome. Some individuals with this syndrome exhibit coprolalia; that is, they frequently make profane or derogatory statements in situations that are not socially appropriate. There are other individuals with this disorder who display a different version of behavioral inhibition. They may not be able to refrain from voicing out loud what they are thinking. As Goldberg (2001) notes: "At times we all have thoughts which social norms prevent us from voicing in public" (p.183). We may notice someone that has a large blemish, birthmark, or a particular disability, but we refrain from mentioning it in their presence. But in some individuals with Tourette's syndrome, this is not the case. It seems like the editor to their thoughts has taken a long lunch break, so to speak. Sometimes, individuals diagnosed with Tourette's may not speak the words; but instead, they pantomime them:

••
Sixteen-year-old William, an individual diagnosed with Tourette's, noticed a girl in his homeroom with protruding teeth. Whenever he saw her, he would immediately make his own teeth visually protrude as if he, too, had this dental malformation. William's teachers had disciplined him for this rude behavior, but he was powerless to stop it.
••

Individuals with Alzheimer's disease frequently experience executive function deterioration in the area of behavioral inhibition as well:

A 75-year-old woman was diagnosed with Alzheimer's. One of the first symptoms her family noticed was her inability to keep her thoughts to herself. She would frequently make derogatory comments about other individuals. This was very uncharacteristic of her interactions prior to the onset of the illness. At a recent family get-together, she was heard to remark that her sister's recipe for pasta salad was terrible and that no one should be eating it if they knew what was good for them.

There are also individuals who exhibit echopraxia; that is, they imitate the actions of others. As an example, if I scratch my nose, an individual with echopraxia would then respond by scratching his. Again, the lack of being able to control this imitative behavior is apparent. As with coprolalia, some individuals with echopraxia know that their behavior is inappropriate, but depending upon the extent of their cognitive impairment, may be powerless to stop it.

In school settings, when teachers and administrators are faced with the behavioral challenges of students with ADHD, Tourette's, or autism spectrum disorders, it sometimes becomes necessary to decide if the challenging behavior should be eliminated through punishment. At such times, educators need to think about whether the challenging behavior is a result of the student's *noncompliance* or because of his/her *incompetence*. There is a difference. If a student with an executive function disorder does not have the supports he needs to be successful in the school environment, he may be demonstrating through his behavior that he is *incompetent*. In such cases, it is not appropriate to discipline the student as a neurotypical child would be disciplined without providing the learning component that he needs to be able to exhibit appropriate behavior in the future:

••

Matthew was a 15-year-old student with ADHD. He was frequently suspended for making terroristic threats when he became angry. The school was considering expelling Matthew due to this behavioral problem. Matthew's parents invited an ADHD consultant to their child's hearing. The consultant reviewed Matthew's IEP and found no evidence that the school was teaching Matthew appropriate ways to manage his anger or express his feelings (i.e. self-regulation skills). The consultant testified at the hearing that Matthew was *incompetent* rather than *noncompliant*, and that until such direct instruction had been supplied to this student in his school setting, the district should not consider expulsion.

••

Behavioral inhibition has been described as occurring in three versions: (1) the ability to stop or inhibit a response before it begins, (2) the ability to stop or inhibit a response that has already begun, and (3) the ability to delay a response until it is more appropriate to begin that response and/or to block interfering or competing events (Bronowski 1977; Fuster 1989). A lack of behavioral inhibition can sometimes be attributed to an inclination to seek out immediate reinforcement. A student who is seeking immediate reinforcement could be demonstrating all three versions as described above. For instance, a child may be impulsive because he wants to obtain what he desires (e.g. escape from work or gain for himself a favorite activity or treat). Such a child is exhibiting behavior that is very much the same as that described in (1), (2), or (3) above. Consider the following example:

••

Colin is working very diligently to complete his math paper. His teacher has promised him that if he completes his paper, he will be able to share in the class treat (candy). Colin sees the treats lying on a desk at the front of the classroom. All at once, he leaves his seat and rushes to the desk to grab

the candy. As he approaches the treats, he is reprimanded for doing so; however, Colin continues his quest for the treats. He returns to his seat, munching the candy, and then refuses to finish his work. Colin has exhibited an inability to inhibit his initial response, inhibit his response once it has already been initiated, and/or delay his response to a more appropriate time (i.e. after he has finished his math). On the positive side, his teachers have identified that candy (treats) are positive reinforcers for Colin. It may be helpful to show Colin a picture of the treat he will earn upon completion of the work instead of having the treat easily accessible to him.
• •

For an educator, the theory that a child will put forth his best efforts to obtain immediate reinforcement is an important consideration when trying to increase a student's level of motivation and avoid behavioral inhibition problems like Colin's. However, the reinforcer will only be effective to motivate or keep a child motivated if it is *reinforcing for the student*. Thus parents and educators should work carefully together to create a menu of reinforcers that their student with executive function deficiency will find reinforcing (Moyes 2002) (see the Worksheet "I Can Choose My Own Rewards"). By allowing the child to select his reinforcers, we have a greater likelihood of the reinforcement program being successful.

In addition, because of the very nature of this cognitive deficit, delaying reinforcement for a future day, or even until the end of a current school day, is most likely not going to be successful for these children who often require immediate gratification for their efforts.

Perseverative behavior is another example of a deficit in behavioral inhibition. Students with this problem have difficulty with both inhibiting a certain behavior and stopping it once it has begun. Such students may appear "hooked" on a certain topic of interest, or a particular behavior:

• •

Courtney is a nine-year-old student with autism. She is an expert on the subject of sea turtles. Her knowledge of sea turtles amazes her teachers as well as the employees and marine biologists at the local zoo. In fact, Courtney was invited to give a presentation about this subject when the zoo's new aquarium opened to the public. Courtney's teachers and parents have decided to forbid her access to materials involving sea turtles in the school setting. They made this decision because this perseverative interest is interfering with Courtney's learning. But even though materials about sea turtles are no longer available to her at school, she frequently attempts to discuss this subject with her peers, and this interferes with their learning as well.

• •

The perseveration may be abnormal in intensity or focus, and sometimes both. In the case above, the interest in sea turtles was abnormal in intensity. Although one would not typically expect a nine-year-old to be so absorbed in the study of sea turtles, the subject matter is not really abnormal. Occasionally, however, the subject of interest is not age-appropriate and is considered abnormal:

• •

Todd is a teen with pervasive developmental disorder. Frequently, Todd engages in discussions about Thomas the Tank Engine. He collects Thomas trains, assembles them, watches Thomas videos, and requests to purchase Thomas the Tank Engine apparel. His family worries about this perseveration, as it is interfering with his ability to interact and engage with peers. He is not interested in other types of trains.

• •

Perseverative behavior is a key symptom of cognitive dysfunction. For children in school, the more severe the cognitive dysfunction, the more likely the child will exhibit perseverative behavior that interferes with his learning:

• •

Angelina was a student with cognitive disabilities. She frequently had difficulty in her math class. Angelina would attempt to solve all math problems from left to right, despite frequent practice and reminding that she needed to utilize a right to left approach. Often times she would appear to finally "get it," only to return to the old way the next time she was asked to solve a problem.

• •

Children with obsessive-compulsive disorder also have deficits in behavioral inhibition. After watching a child with this disability struggle as he washes his hands over and over, one becomes aware of the youngster's inability to inhibit this response due to his anxiety about cleanliness. Or consider the individual who cannot leave the house without checking all the appliances to make sure that they are off. Frequently, he checks them several times, and some days the checking process tacks on an extra 20 minutes to his morning routine and makes him late for work. There may also be times when he returns to the home to make sure these appliances are off. These symptoms may also be present in the young adolescent who lines up her nail polish bottles a certain way on her dresser and gets angry with her mother when she moves them to dust.

Consider, too, the teenager with attention deficit disorder who is accused of stealing another's property. It may very well be that he didn't purposely set out to take the property. But, rather, he could not inhibit the response to take it when it was placed within his line of vision. Such an individual may tell you that it's wrong to steal, but when placed in a situation where the desired article is close at hand, may be unable to resist the temptation to take it.

In school settings, we frequently observe students who eat food from another's plate without permission, get into others' desks, lockers, or backpacks, or even put on someone else's clothing, all because the food or the shoes are in the vicinity of the student. These individuals are at the mercy of their immediate environments. Such behavior can be very frustrating to parents and teachers:

· ·

Alan was a student who participated in a special handwriting class. The teachers frequently used multi-sensory techniques to teach handwriting so that the children would find the learning fun and enjoyable. A can of shaving cream was resting upon a table near Alan. His teacher, knowing that Alan had difficulty controlling his behavior, went to great lengths to explain to Alan that he must not spray the cream and that only his teacher was allowed to use the can. Alan nodded and repeated the rule for the teacher. While the teacher bent down to retrieve a lost pencil, Alan grabbed the can and sprayed it on his face. When the teacher asked Alan what the rule was, he politely explained that only teachers should spray the cream.

· ·

Some behaviorists who work with students who demonstrate behavioral inhibition difficulties feel that teaching the students to delay gratification is a helpful step in normalizing behavioral inhibition tendencies. One such behaviorist uses preferred food items. She places a small piece of candy on the student's desk. She tells the student he can eat the candy right away if he wants. Then she further goes on to say that if he waits five minutes to eat the candy, he will obtain two pieces instead of one. Gradually she increases the increments of wait time by simultaneously increasing the portions of the reward.

She feels that this is a fundamental step in helping students to learn to wait for their reinforcers while doing school work. This is commonly referred to as the Marshmallow Experiment. The Marshmallow Experiment refers to a series of studies that originated in the late 1960s and early 1970s. Preschoolers were presented with the choice of eating a marshmallow right away or waiting. If they could wait, they would receive a second marshmallow. Later studies of these same children indicated that those who could wait had higher IQs, did better on their SAT tests, were socially adjusted, and were able to avoid serious behavior problems, including addictions (Casey *et al.* 2011).

Because having efficient behavioral inhibition mechanisms is so critical to effective cognitive functioning, it is considered by some to be the "king" of the executive functions. In the next chapter, we will continue our study of behavioral inhibition and its effect on learning.

★

Worksheet: "I Can Choose My Own Rewards"

For each possible reward, put a checkmark under the column that most appropriately describes the way you feel about the item. For instance, if having a snack in class is not very important to you, put a checkmark in the "1" column. If it is somewhat important to you, put a checkmark in the "2" column. If it is very important to you, put a checkmark in the "3"

	1	2	3
Snack in class			
Free time			
Listen to music			
Read a favorite book or magazine			
Go to the library			
Take a walk outside			
Swing on the swing set			
Shoot hoops in the gym			
Chocolate			
Computer time			
Play a musical instrument			
Chew gum			
Watch a movie			

	1	2	3
Drink a can of pop			
Play a video game			
Draw			
Write a story			

A Lesson Plan for Teaching Students to Refrain from Negative Words

IEP goal

"Matthew will be able to demonstrate the ability to refrain from the use of negative words with peers during recess in four out of five 15-minute monthly observations."

Supplies needed

- A window screen

- Student worksheet

- Plastic bugs

- A few sticks and leaves

Direct instruction

"Boys and girls, we all have been told that there are certain things that we should not say to someone. These things may hurt someone's feelings. Imagine the screen that you probably have in your window at home. If the window is open without a screen, bugs and debris can come into your home by crawling in or blowing in. But we like to have the breeze flowing into our house that comes when the windows are open." (*Demonstrate debris entering in.*)

"Boys and girls, our brains are like screens. We can let our good words and actions come out, but we should keep our not-so-good words and actions inside. The debris can be compared to our unkind words and the cool air is like our kind words." (*Compare the brain to a "filtering device."*)

Individual worksheet

The next activity involves a list of words or phrases that are both inappropriate and appropriate and two columns that read: "Screen Keeps In" and "Screen Allows Out." Preface having the students do the worksheet with a brief overview that includes general rules to follow with examples. For instance, "You should always avoid the following types of words":

- Curse words

- Self-deprecating words

- Threats

- Insults:

    ❖ negative comments about someone's belongings: "Your purse is ugly!"

    ❖ negative comments about someone's intelligence: "You are so stupid!"

    ❖ negative comments about someone's appearance: "You are so fat!"

    ❖ etc.

When the students begin the worksheet, they will put each word or phrase in the appropriate column. If it is a negative word or phrase, it goes under the "Screen Keeps In—Unkind Words" column. If it is a positive word or phrase, it goes in the "Screen Allows Out—Kind Words" column.

★

Note: This lesson plan can also be adapted for behaviors that are inappropriate as well—for example, engaging in aggressive or dangerous acts, sexually inappropriate behaviors.

Reinforcer

When the student is exhibiting appropriate interactions with peers, he should receive a preferred reinforcer, or a token that earns such a reinforcer. This may include a picture of the reinforcer or a wooden coin to earn increments of it at a later time. Remember, though, that reinforcement is more likely to be effective if it is delivered as soon as possible. When the student is not being appropriate (perhaps he is using unkind words), he could write the word on a piece of paper and put it on the screen. At the end of the day, he can receive a reinforcer based on how many papers are on the screen (the fewer papers, the greater the reinforcer). Discussing each individual paper can also serve as a lesson and a reminder of what kind and unkind words were used and what categories they belonged in.

A Lesson Plan to Teach Students to Refrain from Perseverative Talk

IEP goal

"Matthew will limit talk about _____ (*insert perseverative interest here*) to three opportunities daily and only during appropriate classroom intervals four out of five times weekly."

Supplies needed

- Three 3 x 5 un-ruled cards or pieces of paper
- One lunch-size zip lock baggie
- Marker

Direct instruction

"Sometimes in school, it's important to listen to the teacher. When we are talking about something else, we can't pay attention. For instance, I like to garden. If I talk about gardening instead of listening to the teacher, I won't be able to get my work done. I know that there will be time for me to think about gardening later when I am home, and my work is done. In school, there are times when it's O.K. to talk about _____ (*insert student's perseverative interest here*), and there are times when it isn't." (*Describe times when it's O.K., and when it isn't.*)

★

"Talking about_____ excessively is not O.K. Now, I am going to use the marker to write _____ (*insert student's perseverative interest*) on each card. These cards will help you to remember when it's O.K. to talk about _____ and when it's not." (*Write the student's perseverative topic on each card. For instance, if the student likes to talk about carpenter ants, write "carpenter ants" on each card.*)

"You are going to have the opportunity to talk three times with me today about _____ (*insert student's perseverative interest*), but only when it is appropriate to do so. I will come to you to talk, and it will most likely be during break, at lunch, or recess. If I forget, you can come to me with one of the cards. When you use a card up, we will put it in the zip lock baggie."

"When the baggie is full with all three cards, and you haven't talked about _____ (*insert perseverative interest*) during other times of the day, you will earn some free time at the end of the day to read about _____ (*insert perseverative interest*). If you forget, I will remind you that it's not an appropriate time to talk about _____ and take one of your remaining cards and put it in your baggie. If you have no cards left to take away, you won't earn the extra time at the end of the day to read about _____, but, we can try again tomorrow. Do you understand?"

Note: Remember, the student's perseveration is also likely to be highly reinforcing for him so allowing him to engage in this activity during *appropriate* times and with *limited duration* is important to teach the student that he has to channel his perseveration to appropriate times and with appropriate duration. If the student really struggles with this skill, try shortening the time he has to be appropriate and work up to a full day.

This lesson can also be modified so that the student is allowed to engage in only a limited number of conversation exchanges about the special interest each time he communicates with someone.

CHAPTER FOUR

Behavioral Inhibition, Continued

Perseveration and Shifting

As discussed in Chapter 3, many individuals with executive function deficits have difficulty with behavior that requires them to shift from one activity to another or from one thought process to another. As an example, a young neurotypical student knows that he had a great time playing during recess outdoors with his friends, but now it's time to shift from thoughts of playing outside to thoughts of concentrating on his math papers now that he is inside again and working at his desk. Appropriately stopping one's behavior or "putting on the brakes," is problematic for children with executive function deficits.

As already noted, individuals with obsessive-compulsive disorder exhibit behavioral inhibition difficulties as well. They cannot shift their thoughts away from their obsessions or compulsive behaviors and instead engage in repetitive routines, activities, conversations, or thoughts. So too, individuals with schizophrenia are known to exhibit this cognitive rigidity, as are children with autism spectrum disorders. It is thought by some that the inability to shift may be the reason that individuals with autism often insist on sameness. Indeed, those students who have a greater amount of executive function deficit appear to be those who also have the most difficulty with changes in routine:

• •

Marc, a student with autism, has a lot of difficulty with change. His mother reports that Marc will tantrum if she moves the furniture. Putting up a Christmas tree is particularly difficult for Marc as this means the living room couch needs to be turned a certain way. So too, if Marc is not provided with the same dinnerware each evening, he will refuse to eat.

• •

The above example illustrates how perseverative behaviors can interfere with an individual's ability to complete necessary, everyday tasks. In individuals with perseveration difficulties, there is a lack of the ability to suppress one behavior in favor of beginning or continuing another. When the new behavior is considered to be more socially appropriate than the perseverative behavior, and the child cannot switch to this new behavior, problems will often arise for the child in school and community settings.

Piaget (1954) describes a widely known example of infant perseveration termed the "A-not-B" error. When infants between eight and ten months of age retrieve an object at location A, and then are asked to search for it while it is conspicuously placed in location B, they usually will continue to try to retrieve it at location A. In typical infants, maturity remedies this problem. For children with executive function deficits, maturity will not be enough.

Inflexibility and perseveration are sometimes seen in either the thought processes of children with executive function deficits or in their motor functions. In some children, they can be seen in both. An example would be a student who has learned to form a letter from the top left corner down, but even after multiple practice trials resorts to forming the letter from the bottom left corner up. It will be necessary for such a child's teachers to decide if this is something that really needs to be remediated, or something that should be bypassed in favor of more important goals. It will be important for the teacher to weigh the drawbacks of allowing the student to continue the perserveration versus attempting to eliminate it. For this student who has an executive function disorder, there will probably be far more important deficits to address than how he forms his letters.

As we discussed in Chapter 3, perseveration may prevent a student from inhibiting or stopping a behavior once it has begun. For some students, once a behavior has been activated, it may be quite difficult to stop it. For instance, a child may be asked to repeat once a single nursery rhyme, and then proceed to repeat it over and over again, even when asked to stop. Parents and teachers often refer to students with these issues as "inflexible." For these boys and girls, shifting from one activity (or thought process) to another is extremely difficult. Children with autism spectrum disorders often demonstrate rigidity during times of transition:

••

Elizabeth is a student with high-functioning autism. She is a student in a typical classroom that utilizes learning stations in its reading module. This type of instruction requires Elizabeth to move from one table to another and to initiate and finish a new activity at that table every 15 minutes. Elizabeth becomes very stressed when she must transition. Often her teacher must provide hand-over-hand assistance and actually physically move her to the next activity. Her teachers can assist Elizabeth by providing a transition chart and then rewarding her compliance with a preferred reinforcer as she moves through each station. For instance, her teacher could color-code each station. Elizabeth's order of progression should be presented to her at the outset, along with a color-coded reminder card (similar to a *Candy Land* card) that visually demonstrates for her that she is to move first to yellow, then green, then blue, etc. If she does so successfully, she should earn a preferred reinforcer (in Elizabeth's case, it is Disney princesses, and her teacher provides her with a picture of one if she moves through the transition without resisting or tantruming). Providing her with five-minute warnings prior to each transition would also be helpful.

•••

Research from Dettmer *et al.* in 2000 indicates that in elementary and middle school, visual supports have been shown to reduce transition times and increase performance in the classroom. (See pages 50–51 and Figures 4.1–4.5 on the following pages for other ideas.)

Some children with frontal lobe inadequacy also experience "rule-governed" behavior. This happens when the child perseverates on the rules and expects everyone around him to also devote this kind of attention to them. Difficulty arises when the student is not able to adapt his understanding of the rule to the complexity or social norms of the behavior *in its context.*

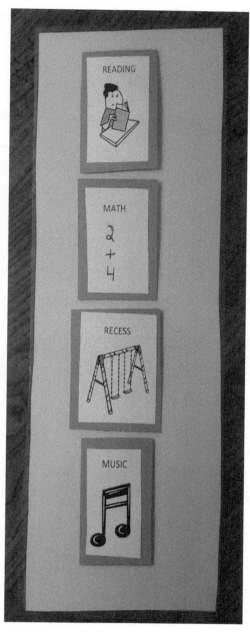

Figure 4.1 Example of a student transition schedule

Figure 4.2 Student transition schedule on a pocket envelope

Figure 4.3 Visual countdown to reinforcement

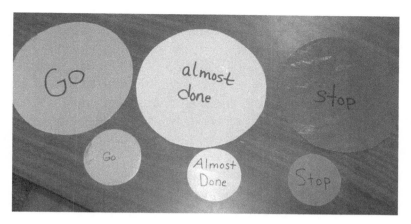

Figure 4.4 Visual for time management

Figure 4.5 IF you can do (math), THEN you can do (cards)

••

Seventeen-year-old Brian is an individual with autism. His parents gave him a motorcycle for his birthday. Brian has a driver's license and knows the motor-vehicle safety code. One day, he drove the bike on a country road at 70+ miles per hour, knowing full well that the speed limit for this particular road was 45 miles per hour. He was pulled over by a patrol man who happened to know Brian's family and that Brian was autistic. He explained to Brian that he was giving him a ticket for speeding at 55 miles per hour in a 45-mile per hour zone. Brian was angry with the officer for not realizing that he was actually driving at 70+ miles per hour. He called the policeman "dumb" for not enforcing the law. Brian's cognitive inflexibility and rule-governed behavior did not allow him to realize that the patrol man was making an exception for Brian's behavior by reducing his ticket fee because he knew Brian's family and because Brian was autistic.

••

Six Ideas to Help with Transitions

- Use a picture schedule to depict the modules of a student's day in pictures. Showing the student in the picture is very helpful. Arrange the pictures on a strip of Velcro.

- Use a timer to depict the amount of time an activity will take before another transition will occur. If the student is bothered by sounds, utilize a soundless timer (e.g. one that uses color or sand to denote the remaining amount of time).

- Make sure to show a way that the activities are finished (e.g. peeling the pictures off the Velcro and putting them inside of an envelope is a good way to show that the activity is completed).

- Give the student a transition item to carry with him as he/she moves through a transition. For instance, as he/she moves to art, give him/her a paint brush to carry.

- Provide transition warning cues at least five minutes before the transition is to occur (dimming the lights, making an announcement, ringing a bell, turning on or off music).

- Allow sufficient time for transition—there's nothing more stressful than not having enough time to move from one place to another or from one activity to another.

Note: In school settings, do not give important information right before or during a transition (such as announcing that there will be a test tomorrow, or announcing the homework assignment for the next day). Most likely, these will be forgotten.

Rule-governed behavior can cause many difficulties in a classroom setting. Children with this executive function deficit can be insistent that teachers enforce their rules. Frequently, they will become known as the "rule policemen" due to their incessant tattling about other students' behavior and their inability to forgive the minor infractions of the rules that all children sometimes make. They may be come frustrated, anxious, and angry at the adults who do not discipline students who break the rules. As one can imagine, this type of behavior does not endear them to their peers! They may even take it upon themselves to become the classroom disciplinarians:

· ·

Five-year-old Robin is often very frustrated in his kindergarten classroom. His teacher had posted a rule chart, but often does not enforce it. One day, a student (Mickey) was repeatedly throwing crayons, despite the fact that the rule chart forbade throwing toys and materials. Robin was becoming increasingly agitated and asked the teacher to make this student stop because he was breaking the rule (and the crayons)! The teacher provided a verbal warning, but this did not eliminate Mickey's behavior. Robin, as a last resort, approached Mickey and hit him over the head. He then announced, "And now I am going to sit in the time-out chair for hitting Mickey." He then went to the time-out chair and sat for the predetermined five minutes that was established for discipline in his classroom.

· ·

We all know of well-meaning teachers and parents who have attempted to help such students by teaching them that "tattling" is inappropriate. But consider the following example:

· ·

Bill is a student with autism. He is experiencing some bullying in the high school setting. Some of this bullying has turned physical and has resulted in torn clothing and even bruises. Bill refuses to point the finger at the students who are doing this to him. When asked why he refuses, he explains patiently that tattling is not appropriate. Apparently, well-meaning teachers in his past have imparted the knowledge to Bill that tattling is wrong. Because of his cognitive rigidity, he cannot shift his belief system and point out the wrongdoers, even when they are causing him bodily harm.

· ·

When a student is unable to be flexible and tolerant with events and people in the world around him, behavioral inhibition difficulties may be the root cause. Teachers and parents need to be aware that an inability to be flexible and tolerant of changing classroom expectations or with gray areas of social conduct may cause a lot of stress for these children. Excessive rigidity about classroom routines, rules, and particular ways of accomplishing tasks brings with it anxiety as these students attempt to cope with the world around them. They may become perfectionistic about their schoolwork, frequently correcting what they perceive as errors, or become greatly distressed when they make mistakes. They may also be unreasonably demanding of themselves:

• •

Nicole is a student with nonverbal learning disability. She is in fourth grade and her parents are reporting that she has low self-esteem. She becomes very upset when reviewing papers that have been graded by her teacher. If she has made any errors, she frequently will break down and cry. Often her completed class papers are filled with erasures because she thinks that she must correct and re-correct her work. She has high expectations for herself, and often resists trying new tasks because she thinks she is "stupid."
• •

For such students, anti-anxiety medications and counseling using a cognitive behavioral approach are frequently recommended. Cognitive behavioral therapy teaches the student new thought patterns. In this way, individuals can not only begin to understand their behaviors but learn replacement skills. Left unchecked, behaviors such as those described above may be precursors to depression.

In evaluating students with possible executive function impairments one of the tools used to measure cognitive flexibility is the Stroop Test (Golden, Freshwater, and Golden

2002). During the evaluation, the student is required to look at a list of color names, but those words are printed in alternative colors. (For instance the word *red* is printed in blue letters.) The evaluator completing this test will first encourage the students to read the words printed on the cards and say the words out loud. Then, the evaluator will change the procedure and have the student say out loud the color of the ink used to print the words. For a child with executive function deficits, it will be extremely hard for him to inhibit the behavior of saying out loud the printed word instead of first examining the ink color of the printed word and saying out loud the ink's color. Indeed, the Stroop Test can be highly effective in identifying children who may have executive function deficits.

Another such test is provided by the Wisconsin Card Sorting Test (Grant and Berg 2003). This test requires the subject to sort cards that have pictures of varying numbers of simple geometric forms (circles, squares, triangles, etc.) into three categories according to a simple rule. This rule is not revealed to the individual being evaluated. He must sort the cards based on what he feels the rule is. Suddenly, the cards are changed, and he must establish a new rule for sorting. Success at this task requires the subject to be flexible as well as to be able to hold the rules for sorting in his working memory.

In summary, what may appear to some as an extreme case of inflexibility or stubbornness, may actually be a sign of an executive function disorder. Educators and parents will need to be flexible as well in their understanding of how these deficits impact on the child's self-esteem, their ability to handle anxiety, and their academic functioning.

A Lesson Plan to Help Rule-Governed Children

IEP goal

"Matthew will reduce the number of tattling occurrences in the classroom from _____ (*insert baseline number of occurrences here*) to no more than _____ per week. In addition, he will be able to distinguish when it is O.K. to tattle and when it is not."

Supplies needed

- Blackboard and chalk or whiteboard and markers

Direct instruction

"Boys and girls, there is one person in charge of the classroom, and that is the teacher. The teacher makes the rules and enforces the rules. I am the teacher in this classroom. Let's list some rules for my classroom." (*Begin to take suggestions and write these on the board.*)

"Sometimes, in the course of a school day, you may notice that some students break the rules. Most likely, you will break a few too. The teacher in the classroom is in charge of the discipline. If he/she wants to discipline a student for breaking the rules, he/she can. If he/she does not want to discipline a student for breaking the rules, he/she can do that too. It is not the students' job to tell the teacher about other students who are breaking rules. This is called "tattling." When students tattle, it frequently upsets the student who is being tattled on.

"Now, let's look at all of the rules on the board. Let's put a check mark beside the ones that, if broken, could cause someone to be hurt or injured." (*One by one, review the rules and write a check mark next to those that have the potential to cause injury or harm to another person.*)

"There are some rules here that it's O.K. to tattle to the teacher about. In fact, if someone is getting hurt or could get hurt, you should tell the teacher. The rules that we have checked are the ones that it would be O.K. to tattle about."

"There's one other thing we should discuss, and that is 'how' to tattle. It is best to talk to the teacher privately, or to raise your hand and talk to him/her quietly rather than to tattle out loud. It's not everyone else's business to hear that someone is breaking a rule."

"Beginning today, if you feel the need to tattle, please look at this list and decide if it is a rule that you should tell the teacher about or not. If it is, raise your hand and speak to the teacher (me) quietly. If it is not, you should ignore the behavior and let the teacher handle it in his or her own way."

Note: At this point, it might be helpful to have various scenarios to review to see if the students can apply the procedure of whether they should or should not tattle, based on the example provided.

In addition to the direct instruction, it may be helpful to offer reinforcers for students who refrain from tattling and apply the procedure correctly.

CHAPTER FIVE

Theory of Mind

Theory of mind is often referred to as the ability to understand others as intentional agents; that is, to take another individual's beliefs into account and to appreciate how they might be different from one's own. But going one step further, theory of mind is the ability to understand how someone else feels and why. With this knowledge, an individual can then adjust his or her behavior appropriately. Theory of mind can also be described as the ability to know what someone else knows. Part of that knowledge is in being able to "read" how the individual feels and to keep track of what he/she knows to make accurate judgments:

••

Jarrod, a student with autism, has difficulty with perspective-taking. This causes him to act inappropriately in social situations because he cannot "read" the social cues. Jarrod's parents recently shared that Jarrod was engaging in a conversation about the benefits of being an atheist with a neighbor who was known to be very active in her local Catholic church. If Jarrod was able to read her body language, he would have been aware that she was very offended at his choice of topics. Jarrod would then be able

to refrain from engaging in such topics of conversation in the future when conversing with this neighbor.
••

Children with frontal lobe deficiency will most often need to learn social skills using a direct instruction approach. If a child with these deficits is to learn perspective-taking skills, a hierarchy of social skills instruction needs to be provided which includes:

- Tier I: teaching eye contact and joint attention skills (sharing and engaging in activities together)

- Tier II: explicit instruction in recognizing facial expressions using a wide variety of models to encourage generalization

- Tier III: instruction and practice in learning to read body language also from a variety of models

- Tier IV: direct instruction with the student to dissect social scenarios where the characters must implement various strategies by weighing out the social consequences associated with each.

Research completed by Pamela Crooke, Ryan Hendrix, and Janine Rachman in 2008 indicates that after structured treatment and generalization practice, children with autism spectrum disorder showed significant increases in appropriate social behavior.

Having good theory of mind is much more than being able to take perspectives. We know that theory of mind develops in very young children:

••

Todd was a four-year-old child with autism spectrum disorder. He wanted to trick-or-treat at his grandparents' home. His father called his grandparents and told them that when they opened the door, Todd would be dressed as a tiger. He asked that the grandparents pretend that they didn't know who Todd was. Because Todd did not possess good theory of mind, he assumed that his grandparents would not know who he was in his tiger costume, even though his parents were also at the door without costumes.

••

Many professionals in the psychological field have expressed their frustration over the lack of evaluation tools that can be used to assess theory-of-mind skills. Many of these instruments are currently being developed, or are not readily available. There are a few that researchers are beginning to use as of the publication date of this book. Let's discuss a few of these now.

In tests of false belief, the student must predict what a story character's response will be given the character's mistaken beliefs about the social situation occurring. There are first-order tests (Marge thinks that …) and there are second-order tests (Marge thinks that Bryan thinks that …). Some children with mild executive function deficits are able to complete first-order theory-of-mind tests successfully, but then have difficulty with second-order tests. In the "Sally–Anne" test, developed by Wimmer and Perner in 1983, two puppets, Sally and Anne, "act" out a skit for the student being evaluated. "Sally" puts a marble in a basket and leaves the room. "Anne" takes the marble out and moves it to another location. When "Sally" returns, where will be the first place she looks for her marble? Individuals with theory-of-mind deficit will often say that "Sally" will look in the second location.

Another type of assessment that is useful for determining if a child is exhibiting theory-of-mind deficits are cartoon tests (Corcoran, Cahill, and Frith 1997). The student is asked to study cartoons depicting characters demonstrating various mental states and physical states. Again, some students are able to look at the cartoon and decipher the character's physical state, but then have immense difficulty interpreting the character's mental state.

In reading assignments, when children are presented with stories or cartoons where the protagonist says things that are not true for a variety of different motivations (sarcasm, white lies, etc.), children with executive function deficits are often unable to offer an explanation as to why the character said what he said. Thus, the students' grades often reflect difficulty with inferential type reading.

The Advanced Theory-of-Mind Test (Happé 1994) assesses a child's higher level theory-of-mind skills using nonliteral language. For instance, the child may read a mental state story and the main character will say something that may contain sarcasm. The child must then offer a response as to why the character said what he/she did. Typically children with executive function deficits are known to have difficulty with sarcasm:

••

Joey, a nine-year-old boy with autism, was being educated alongside neurotypical peers in a regular education classroom. Joey's teacher, a young man in his 20s, often used sarcasm as a way of relating to his charges. One day, Joey came to class wearing a new neon green shirt. His teacher remarked "I see Joey's mom failed to turn on the lights when she went to the store and bought *that* shirt!" Joey looked confused and said, "But all the stores have lights so that people can see when they shop. Don't you know that?"

••

A measure of true theory-of-mind skills is not based on whether the student can decipher sarcasm or understand nonliteral language such as idioms and figures of speech. Theory-of-mind deficits arise when the student is unable to decipher or determine what *someone else* is thinking. Thus, true theory-of-mind evaluations should tap whether a child can correctly describe what someone else is thinking about or feeling. The game of chess or checkers, according to Goldberg (2001), is a concrete example of theory-of-mind skills and how they interact with executive functions. The players must make their moves based on what they think the other players will do. A player must weigh out various test options in his mind, before he ever moves a pawn, and evaluate the consequences of each. He must form a plan and not move his pieces haphazardly if he going to win the game.

When a person has insight into other people's thoughts, he generally is perceived as "socially smart." Often these individuals lead successful lives in sales or as corporate or political leaders. They are personable. They are experts at reading what other people may be thinking and then flexible in adapting their behavior and/or words accordingly. Successful politicians are adept at crafting their words so that distinct opposing opinions feel that the politician is "on their side." In contrast, individuals with frontal lobe deficiencies often find themselves unable to navigate such intricate social interactions appropriately.

Many times, individuals with executive function deficits are perceived to be selfish, egocentric, and antisocial. Since they lack the ability to take on others' perspectives, they will appear to be unsympathetic or uncaring. Members of our society are somewhat forgiving when it comes to social behavior breaches of individuals presumed to have disabilities. The problem with this, however, is that individuals with executive function deficits are often not readily identified as individuals with disabilities.

★

A Lesson Plan to Help Teach Theory of Mind

IEP goal

"Mary will be able to recognize and label how various people may be feeling in pictures and offer a corresponding comment in 18 out of 20 tries."

Supplies needed

- Pictures from magazines or the internet of people displaying various emotions

These pictures should be glued to a piece of paper large enough to draw a conversation bubble from their mouths so that the student can write in the bubble which extends from the picture to the paper. If you want to use the pictures again, laminate the entire paper. The students can then use a dry erase, fine-tip marker to write in the conversation bubbles you will draw later in this lesson. You will be able to wipe these off and use them again.

Direct instruction

"Today we are going to discuss various emotions. In order to have meaningful friendships and/or relationships with other people, it's important that you be able to understand how people are feeling. Let's see how well you can do this activity:" (*One by one, show the pictures to the student and have him/her say in two or three words how the person in the picture is feeling. In other words, he/she should be able to recognize and label the emotion of the person in the picture. If the student has immense difficulty with this activity, it may be that he/she must learn to read faces first. If that is the case, a lower-level activity of simply having the student label basic emotions in lots of models (pictures, video samples, software, real-life, etc.) will be a more attainable activity.*

"Now, I am going to show you the pictures again, and I want you to think about WHY the person may be feeling that way. If someone looks sad in the picture, tell me one reason why he/she may be sad—maybe he lost his dog, maybe his favorite toy broke, etc. Let's try!"

(One by one, show the pictures to the student again and have him/her describe in a short sentence a plausible reason why the person in the picture may be depicting that emotion.)

"O.K. When you read comic books, sometimes the characters in the comic strips are saying things. What they say is written in the bubble that comes out of their mouths. This is called a conversation bubble. Now, I am going to show you the pictures again. I want you to write a short phrase or sentence in the bubble—something that is appropriate to the emotion the character is displaying." *(Draw a conversation bubble from the character's mouth that extends onto the paper so that the student can write in the bubble.)*

Note: The only wrong answers would be if a student could not read the individual's emotion and wrote a sentence in the bubble that was not appropriate based on that emotion. It may be helpful to do a few of the cards with the student at first. You may need to provide some direct instruction about what eyebrows do when they are surprised, happy, angry, etc., or what mouths do when they are smiling or sad, etc. to encourage the student to choose appropriate answers. You can also give a reminder of how he/she previously labeled the character's emotion so that he/she can choose appropriate comments.

CHAPTER SIX
Working Memory

Teachers and parents of students with executive function deficits often complain that the student "can't remember" things. He has difficulty keeping information that he has been recently exposed to readily accessible. He may struggle with remembering the steps of processes he has been repeatedly taught.

Working memory is memory that is stored for a very short time, usually somewhere between a few seconds to about a minute while it is used and acted upon. Storage space is limited to about seven thoughts (Miller 1956). The brain must then dismiss the information as not worthy of saving (similar to your "delete" button and emptying your "recycle bin"), or transferring it to long-term memory. For example, working memory enables you to dial a phone number someone just told you. It allows you to remember the driving directions you were just given when you stopped at a gas station because you were lost. Working memory helps you to derive meaning from text that you are reading by assisting you in remembering what was previously read, and it allows you to go to the grocery store for four items without a list. Because the information is readily available, it is much easier to access than information we have stored in long-term memory.

Having good working memory can be compared to sifting through sand to find a lost ring—the brain must sort through and find the one item stored in billions of bits of memory that is needed to solve problems, and this must all happen within a reasonable period of time. Many of us have experienced not being able to recall something when we needed it, but, hours later, we can access it. It is the frontal lobes that help us to hold some granules of information in the forefront because it is anticipated that this particular information will be needed soon, or these granules may be examined briefly and sent back to their designated locations once they have been determined to be unusable.

As a visual for comparison, if one imagines a water pitcher as the amount of working memory a "neurotypical" person has, then a water glass may be the amount of working memory a person with executive function deficits may have.

It is believed that a hierarchy exists within the levels of short-term (working) memory. On the lowest level is sensory memory. Sensory memories are held very briefly (just a few seconds) and appear to be a type of "awareness" to help keep our bodies regulated. For instance, our lips are dry, and we say to ourselves, "I think I'm getting thirsty. I need to go and get a drink." Some researchers feel that sensory memory is merely a recording device and is not truly a function of memory.

The next level of memory is called immediate memory. Its role is to temporarily hold information retained from the registration process, and it lasts from about 30 seconds up to a few minutes. In a school setting, the instructions that are delivered right before a student begins a test are often important ones! As the teacher announces, "Use 'T' for True and 'F' for False," a student with executive function deficits may not have adequate immediate memory skills to recall these instructions in immediate memory.

Next on the hierarchy is rehearsal memory, which is thought to last for hours. This type of memory is activated by rehearsing, or repeating, a series of statements or actions which will enhance and lengthen the ability to save the information and retrieve it later. When we rehearse, we increase the likelihood that information will be stored successfully for later retrieval. For example, rehearsing how you will answer questions in an interview is helpful several hours before the interview actually takes place. Or, after stopping for directions, rehearsing them by chanting the steps to yourself several times may help you recall them as you drive.

Last in the short-term memory hierarchy is long short-term memory. It lasts from an hour to up to approximately two days. It is an intermediate step in transitioning from short-term into long-term (permanent) memory. One can increase the ability to hold information in long-term short memory by the use of mnemonic devices such as phrases or sayings to preserve the memory trace even longer. For instance, how many of us can still remember the order of lines on a music staff by reciting the phrase "Every Good Boy Does Fine" (EGBDF)? This is an example of a mnemonic device, and there are many being used with great success in schools today.

We forget 90 percent of what is learned in classrooms within the first 30 days, and we lose the majority of it within the first few hours after the class is over. If educators want to foster a student's memory recall, they need to repeat important points less than 30 seconds after they are delivered, and then again within the next hour. Over time, these same key points should be continually reviewed. When you learned your address or birthday, it's because you had to repeat it multiple times over the years.

For many in the field of education, memory is a term explained by one's ability to recall information previously committed, and it may be assessed by having the student memorize certain facts and then recall them later. But, in most real-life situations, information is not merely recalled by rote.

It is recalled and used to solve problems. Therefore, we must not only teach our students to recall information, but they must also be taught to apply it. As an example, memorizing that there are 12 phyla in the kingdom Plantae will most likely not be useful to the student because this type of rote information probably will not be able to be recalled once the exam is over, must less 30 days later. If we want to remember the information, we must find ways to connect it to particular sensory activities for the student.

According to Baddeley (1996), "Working memory consists of a central executive, a phonological loop, and a visuo-spacial sketchpad" (p.5). The phonological loop is sound-based; that is, it acts strictly on sounds that must be committed to memory. The visuo-spacial sketchpad acts on information that is visual or spacial. Baddeley informs us that the central executive coordinates both. According to Allan Paivio's dual coding theory (1971), memory is improved when information is presented verbally and visually.

If we use this information to design interventions for children who have difficulty with working memory, we may discover that providing children with memory devices that involve songs, chanting, or visual and tactile experiences may improve working memory because these activities provide a "bookmark" for the student in his brain.

As stated earlier, many music teachers inform us that when helping children to learn the music staff, they utilize the memory phrase "Every Good Boy Does Fine." Because of this one memory phrase, students can often recite the lines on the music staff years later (EGBDF). This "bookmark" enables the child to remember the important information years later.

In typical elementary schools, spelling is often taught by utilizing a rote practice method: students write the words several times to commit them to memory. But using Baddeley's information, it might be more beneficial to have the students learn the words by chanting or using a visual method such as tracing the words in colored powder or sand, or using bendable pipe cleaners to spell the words. Remember, too, that there is research to support that learning and studying in the presence of a particular scent may actually improve a person's ability to recall that information. That's because scent and memory are frequently connected. (Can you recall the smell of your favorite place?)

Many parents ask if their child's working memory size can be improved. It's probably best to look at working memory as something that can be improved by *accommodating the child's learning styles or learning preferences.* In other words, if your child appears to be a tactile learner, than involve him in tactile learning experiences. If he likes to be active and prefers to move about, create studying opportunities that involve movement. Realize, too, that trying to commit to memory important information is very difficult when there are competing or distracting forces in the environment. This is particularly true for children with executive function deficits. Limiting distractions improves attention.

The interventions in the box that follows are ones that need to be considered for use in the IEP (Individualized Education Plan) or the child's 504 plan (list of accommodations educators will provide to ensure the student has equal access to the process of learning).

IEP and 504 Accommodations and Specially Designed Instruction Items for Students with Working Memory Deficits

- Reduce the number of choices in multiple-choice questions. Students may not be able to hold more than three at a time.

- Write and say directions to complete assignments and tests.

- Create a checklist or "to-do" list of steps to follow to solve problems and complete tasks.

- Use multi-sensory instruction to teach required information—opportunities to see, smell, touch, and move.

- Picture lists, cues, and schedules help children to hold upcoming transition information in working memory so that transitions and changes to routine are not as difficult. "Explaining" such changes is not as effective.

- Create rhymes, songs, chants, poems, etc., of important information that must be committed to memory.

- Utilize "chunking"—introducing smaller pieces at a time—separated by breaks (e.g. cutting a worksheet or test in half and having the student complete each part with a break in between).

- Make lectures less wordy and more interactive.

- Announce homework assignments at the start of the period instead of the end—often the end of the period is accompanied by many distractions, such as ringing bells and increased student activity.

- Create "tickler" systems for students—calendars, checklists, email reminders, technology "helpers."

- Incorporate rewards for students who are able to remember required items but don't punish those who can't.

CHAPTER SEVEN

Organizational Skills, Time Management, Planning, and Decision Making

What parent or teacher of a child or student with ADD or ADHD has not complained about his organizational skills? How many extra times has a parent of such a child had to return to the school to search for missing items or retrieve needed books/supplies to complete homework?

The above are common complaints with regard to children who have executive function deficits. These children simply can't seem to remember what it is they need, complete tasks without prompting or multiple reminders, adhere to deadlines, or keep an orderly environment (desk, locker, room, closet). Many adults in these kids' lives adopt an authoritative response as a means of handling these frustrating behaviors. They may withhold snacks, recess, favorite toys, or activities as a punishment for their lack of organizational skills. What adults in these situations end up doing, however, is punishing *incompetence.* Children with executive function deficits have a genuine problem with staying organized, and it's not a choice. Such children must be supported to accomplish these challenging tasks. They need to be taught a "process" to stay organized. In general, students need to be able to organize several aspects of their lives:

- their work and living spaces

- their time (sometimes referred to as time management)

- the work and materials required to complete a task.

It is helpful if teachers and parents provide visual supports to assist a student with the above, as often words may not be enough. Frequently, many children with executive function problems also have language deficits. Thus, delivering all organizational strategies verbally is not going to be effective. For some children, the visual models and examples will make the difference.

As a comparison, many of us cannot buy our groceries without a list. If we leave the list at home, we will most often forget many of the needed items we intended to buy. This visual tool is something that most of us will need each and every time we go to the grocery store for more than a few items because our short-term memories are not effective without it.

Now, let's discuss that a little more. If someone disciplined us for forgetting certain grocery items, it would not improve our ability to be organized in the grocery store. After all, as we have seen, our short-term memories are only so big! And yet, this sort of thing happens every day in schools across the country. Students with genuine executive function difficulties are told that teacher-made visual supports promote dependency, are not appropriate for middle school and high school, and/or that they must develop their own supports.

However, even the process of developing some of these visual supports requires the successful interaction of many executive functions that these children lack!

Sometimes parents and schools take the opposite approach: they begin to enable students and "do the thinking for them." This too is not teaching the student a process to become self-sufficient. One of the most frequent arguments centers around homework:

••

John was a student with executive function deficits. Frequently, he would forget to write down his homework assignments and/or to bring the necessary books home to do those assignments. His teacher decided that the best way to handle the situation was to write his assignments down and pack his needed books in his book bag for him. His parents were thrilled that John's teacher had decided to assist him in this way because frequently they found themselves driving to school to get textbooks or calling his classmates to figure out what it was he had to do for homework.

••

The above scenario is an example of enabling. John must be taught a process to pack his book bag and keep an accurate planner. Otherwise, he will become dependent on the adults in his environment to do this for him. A process could consist of a checklist, a planner, or technology that can help him be better at completing this task. Perhaps a "buddy" can work with him to pack his bag and provide some prompts for him: "Do we have math homework tonight? Do you need your math book?"

Some teachers will provide the family with an extra set of textbooks for the student to keep at home. This, too, could be enabling the student if he is not required to pack his own books as well. A better way to handle this may be providing the extra set, but then encouraging the student to pack his bag, just like the other students. If he is able to bring the correct books and assignments home, his parents should provide a preferred reinforcer. This will serve as an incentive to help the student learn a replacement skill.

Another way to teach a process is through the use of video or pictures. A video-model of how to clean a bedroom or a desk drawer can be extremely helpful. Video-models are short videos that show the steps to completing a task, and they are very useful. A "before" and "after" photo of the task can also be helpful (see Figures 7.1 and 7.2). Some children will have difficulty accomplishing a task with just the "before" and "after" photos to refer to. It may be useful to divide the task into smaller "chunks" with photos of each "chunk." As an example, showing the student the inside of a messy desk vs. a clean desk may not be enough to help him keep a clean desk. He may need pictures of various steps to complete so that he is able to accomplish a replica of the photo of the clean desk.

Figure 7.1 Before

Figure 7.2 After

For many middle and high school students, keeping an orderly locker can also be a challenge. There are lots of useful and decorative items that can be purchased to assist in this process (extra shelving, erase boards, Velcro pouches, etc.), but educators and parents need to keep in mind the reason for these: students with organizational problems need to create less physical chaos for themselves—it is difficult to locate and find materials in a pile of clutter. "Chunking" free areas of space (providing smaller areas to contain supplies in) is useful. As an example, drawer organizers, labeled plastic containers with lids, extra shelving, etc., are all ways to "chunk" free space so that it is not so overwhelming to students.

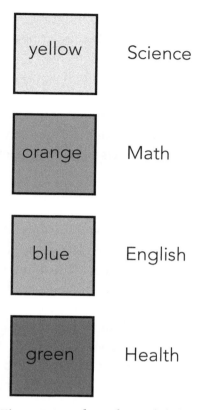

Figure 7.3 Locker color-coded chart

Occasionally, finding one book in a locker of several can be hard too. I recommend covering the books with plain colored cloth book jackets, one color per subject. Purchasing a similarly colored two-pocket folder can be helpful to store papers for that subject. Additionally, three-hole punching these same folders and keeping them in a three-ring binder will help the student have all needed papers readily available. To assist the student in remembering the colors, create a color-code chart on the locker door similar to Figure 7.3. The student, as he goes to math, simply grabs the red book and the corresponding red two-pocket folder because red was the color designated for math.

Organization of free space is not the only type of challenge for students with executive function deficits. Organization of work (planning and time management) is another. Parents often complain that if they did not get involved with the process of completing projects for school, they would never get done.

Some younger children have difficulty completing daily routines such as bathing, dressing, making the bed, etc. Older children and adolescents may show evidence of organizational difficulties by exhibiting a tendency to procrastinate the actual initiation of daily routines. Scheduling the child's time (dinner, homework, free time, bedtime, etc.) using a visual tool will enable the student to learn to be independent but provide him with needed supports. Using a timer and a reward system is helpful for some individuals. As an example, if I am able to complete my work by 8:30 p.m., I will earn a reinforcer of my choice. Breaking routine tasks down into visual checklists can also guide a child through the steps that need to be accomplished to finish a task. Having the child check off each task as he/she completes the list provides him/her with a sense of accomplishment and enables the child to see that there is a clear beginning and a clear end to the task at hand. For some individuals, "chunking" the tasks with break time will be necessary as sitting for extended times is not productive for him/her.

The same problems that a student may exhibit at home are often evident at school as well. When faced with a project, the student may struggle with how to break or "chunk" the task into pieces and how to complete those particular pieces by certain due dates. It is imperative that teachers "check in" with such students to make sure they are on track with completing the project. Establishing intermittent due dates for particular "chunks" of the project will help keep the student working towards completion. The Worksheet "Planning My Project" at the end of this chapter shows the use of a project plan form to complete a long-term project in the school setting. Project plan forms are excellent examples of specially designed instruction items that can be added to the IEP or 504 plan.

In school settings, many of these children also struggle with written expression assignments as well. A thought organizer (often called a graphic organizer) is extremely beneficial in the planning process. We have already discussed how difficult some tasks may be if they contain heavy working-memory demands. Written expression assignments are examples of such tasks. A student must hold the topic and the plan in his/her mind if he/she is to complete it as a coherent, well-organized product. For some students, even developing a step-by-step plan is extremely difficult. Many students will attempt to avoid this type of assignment and be labeled by their teachers as unmotivated. For some, extreme behaviors (crying, elopement, aggression) may also be evident. Often these students struggle with other difficulties as well as executive function deficit that may make written expression tasks extremely challenging: fine motor weaknesses, sensory processing difficulties, language impairment, are examples. Without accommodations, students will shut down and not be able to complete the assignment. Graphic organizers are helpful for many other types of assignments. They support executive function deficit. A useful website where one can obtain hundreds of free graphic organizers can be found at www.freeology.com. An example of a graphic organizer is shown in Figure 7.4. In this example, the student uses each petal of the flower to list different characters in this novel and note some of the personality traits of each character. They can then use the organizer to help them predict what each character might do next.

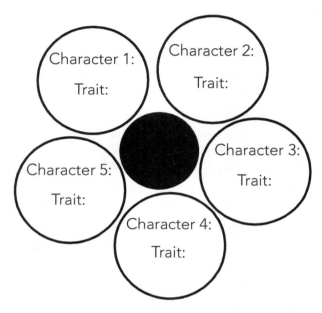

Figure 7.4 Flowers in the Attic by Dollanger

At this point, it is necessary to discuss decision-making skills. Decision making is often extremely difficult for our students with executive function deficits. They do best when choices are limited to only a few. When one must review a variety of choices, it becomes a working-memory struggle as he attempts to hold all choices in his mind and then make the best one. If a child is unable to shift away from a current activity and begin a new task, and if that new task involves making a choice, he will often display oppositional-defiant type behaviors. Refusing to do the new task may certainly be an end-result of a student's way to handle this difficulty. This is another reason why a visual transition schedule is helpful.

If the student knows that a new activity is coming up, he may be less likely to tantrum.

If a teacher is working with a student who is accomplishing very little work because of refusal, chances are that student would do best with limited choices and giving him some "power." That would include allowing him to choose between tasks and including choices with less demand. A two-pocket folder with a task the other students are doing in one pocket (assigned a star-value of three stars) and in the other pocket, a task with much less demand (assigned a star-value of one star) will allow the student to visually see his choices (see Figure 7.5). If he completes the one-star item, he earns a star on his star chart. If he completes the three-star item, he earns three stars on his star chart. The choice is the student's, and the decision he makes has its own set of reinforcers. The more work the student completes, the quicker he can earn a reinforcer that he has selected.

Figure 7.5 Two-pocket folder with starred tasks

Some staff members object that this student is able to earn reinforcers with minimal work. But, when compared to the amount of work this same student previously completed, this method may be helpful to avoid refusal and help to set him on the right path. Gradually the work requirements can increase to earn the preferred reinforcers (one- and three-star tasks). Lastly, it is important to remember that the three-star work item should be appropriately adapted according to the IEP or 504 plan. Many students refuse to do work because it is simply out of the scope of their ability level. Educators must adapt work so that it is appropriate for the students. Otherwise, problem behaviors and anxiety levels will most likely escalate.

Worksheet: Planning My Project

Today's Date _____ Due Date _____

1. What will the end project look like or be?

   _____

2. How much of my grade is it worth?

   _____

3. Will I work alone or with others on the project?

   _____

4. If with others, who are the others?

   _____

5. What is the project title?

   _____

Steps to Completing Project	Due Dates

★

Add initials (if a group project) to determine whose responsibility each item is.

6. List supplies that will need to be obtained or purchased:

_____

_____

_____

CHAPTER EIGHT

Initiation and Motivation

"Class, this afternoon, I am going to allow one hour for you to begin work on your history project for the Civil War time period. Yesterday, I shared with you some projects that other students have completed for this assignment in the past. It was my hope that these projects would spark some ideas of your own. I will circulate the class during this time period and speak with each of you about your own plans. You may begin." Ms. Staton then began to circulate her class, stopping at each student's desk to assess their preliminary plans.

"Matthew, what idea do you have for this project?" Ms. Staton asked.

"I don't know," Matthew answered quietly.

"You mean to tell me you have been sitting here all this time and you can't come up with one idea to use?"

"I just can't think of anything."

"Matthew, this won't do at all. You are going to have to get motivated."

Matthew's teacher may be confusing motivation with initiation. Although many children with executive function deficits appear to lack motivation; in actuality, it may be that they lack the ability to initiate. When a child can initiate a task, he is goal-directed; that is, he has the ability to see the goal in his mind and begin work so that he can accomplish it. But, if he has working memory deficits, he may not even be able to hold the goal in his mind so that he *can* initiate the task.

The field of applied behavior analysis informs us that if want to teach a child to initiate, he should be reinforced for his actual and approximate attempts at this activity. Any behavior that is reinforced is likely to continue (Cooper, Herron, and Heward 2007). Thus, from the standpoint of a behaviorist, often it is as simple as finding a reinforcer that is reinforcing *for the student* and applying this reinforcer frequently at his/her approximations of initiation until initiation behaviors have been successfully shaped for him or her. As an example, if Margo is unable to get started, her teacher could prompt her and say, "I see that you are thinking about what to do first, and that's a good thing, so I am going to put a sticker on your chart. What would be the next thing you should do?"

The above educator may offer another step to help Margo. She has probably recognized her inability to initiate and may instead provide the student with a task organizer—a list of steps the student should follow to begin a task. Perhaps another reinforcer is imbedded within the list, or provided to the student at the completion of the list. For some students, this method may help accomplish more goal-directed activity.

Another method of teaching the skill of initiation is to provide direct instruction through use of a memory device such as "TWINK":

Think about the task

Write three steps to begin the task:

1.

2.

3.

Begin or **I**nitiate the first step.

Begin the **N**ext step.

Keep going.

The teacher may provide direct instruction to the student in the use of TWINK, and then in future lessons, she can cue the student to various parts of TWINK.

But let's discuss motivation. As stated earlier, many educators equate a student's inability to get started with a motivation problem. If you have provided ways (see above) for the student to successfully initiate tasks, then it will be important to consider (especially if the student is still unable to get started) if he is actually motivated to do the work. Motivation is also an executive function. But, it is intricately intertwined with the ability to actually *do the task*.

In schools throughout our country, children with disabilities are often included in typical classrooms. The Individuals with Disabilities Education Act (IDEA) supports the idea that typical peers often serve as positive role models for students with disabilities and thus their achievements are more apt to be imitated. In other words, children with disabilities can make more progress when they have opportunities to learn alongside children without disabilities, and more importantly, they deserve these opportunities. But, IDEA also states that children with disabilities should have accommodations and adaptations to be able to cope in such an environment. When they see their own work products as compared to those of their peers, children with disabilities can become extremely frustrated and stressed, often resulting in depression and lowered self-esteem. This is particularly true when they are required to complete work at levels much higher than their ability level:

•••

Ian was an eighth-grade student with moderate cognitive impairment in an inclusion program at a local middle school. According to school district records, he was a third-grade reader. He was included in all classes with regular education students. In two of his classes, there was a special education teacher present who co-taught with the regular education teacher. He did reasonably well in those classrooms, but his mother reported that his stress level was elevated. In three of his other classes, there was no special education teacher present. Ian was expected to complete all classroom work, outside assignments, and tests, just as his other classmates were. *None of these assignments were adapted to his ability level, and Ian had significant difficulty even reading the textbook.* At the start of the school year, when Ian would raise his hand and ask for help, his teacher would often become frustrated. Now, Ian rarely asks for help, and frequently he will put his head down and refuse to do the work. Ian sees a therapist and takes medication for depression and anxiety.

•••

Clearly, in the above scenario, Ian's placement in an inclusive classroom is not working to his benefit. Sadly, with the increased pressure on educators to meet the high standards of proficiency that their states have enacted for their students, this scenario is not a rare occurrence. Children with disabilities are not getting the accommodations and adaptations they need in order to be successful. Ian expresses his frustration by shutting down. But, there will be other students who become disruptive and possibly aggressive. When examining motivation, it is critical that we also look closely at the tasks we are asking our students to do. Are they suitable in terms of the reading level of our students? Are the working-memory demands needed to complete the assignment acceptable for this student? Do they need to be chunked?

Assuming, however, that the tasks are at an appropriate instructional level, when students exhibit work refusal, we can begin to think about the two levels of motivation and try to ascertain at which of these levels our student is operating from (see below). At first, our goal will be to have Ian initiate and finish tasks. Then, our goal can broaden to include initiating and finishing tasks at a particular level of accuracy and at a certain speed.

- *Intrinsic motivation* describes a student who is motivated to get good grades, to complete the task to the best of his ability level, or to improve his own personal performance. He may feel competition from peers and desire to be "the best." He may want to please his teacher or his parents. As an example, we are intrinsically motivated if we refuse to call off work, even when we are sick, because we would let down "the team" and/or leave them short-staffed.

- *Extrinsic motivation* describes a student who is unwilling to work unless he "gets something" for doing it. Maybe his parents have promised to buy him the latest technology device, or some other tangible reward. For us, if we go to work primarily to earn a paycheck, we are extrinsically motivated.

As educators, we should evaluate at which of the two levels our students are working from, and then meet them at that level. For some of us, this is a hard concept to endorse. Some educators feel that all children should be intrinsically motivated and do not understand the reason for supplying reinforcers (rewards). They have difficulty rationalizing why Sally gets a stick of gum for completing a worksheet, and

Johnny does not. They feel that supplying rewards to certain children and not others is "not fair." Realizing that all children should get what they need in the classroom to perform at their optimal ability level is the ultimate goal: this is what's "fair" to everyone.

Discovering what reinforcers are useful to particular students can be a difficult process. Some students respond to rewards fairly easily; for others, it is a process to locate meaningful reinforcers. Some children respond to praise (see box "25 Ways to Praise a Student" on the following page), others do not. A reinforcer survey (see the worksheet on page 93) is often helpful in ascertaining particular student interests. Educators can also develop their own list of reinforcers, similar to a menu (see Chapter 3), that they are willing to utilize in the classroom. These can then be ranked in order of preference by the students. For some children, rewards will need to be changed frequently to maintain effectiveness. For others, this will not be the case. Food and drink items are usually helpful for students who don't respond well to typical reinforcers. In states where food and drink items are prohibited by state law (or even by school district policy), writing such items in the IEP or 504 plan can supersede these regulations, as IEP and 504 plan accommodations are governed by federal law. It is helpful to have the student "choose" a reinforcer or a picture of a reinforcer that he is working for. The amount of work or the number of tasks that he has to complete to earn it should also be clear to him. Using a visual chart depicting this can be helpful (Figure 8.1).

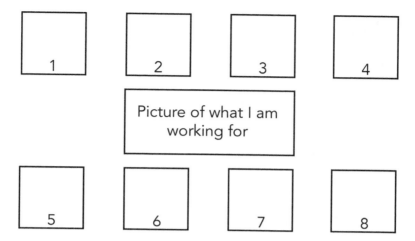

Figure 8.1 Reinforcer chart

25 Ways to Praise a Student

- High five

- Great job

- Knuckle bump

- Fantastic

- Super duper work

- Exceptional job

- You are awesome

- Easy-peasy

- You are on top of the world

- I am so proud of you

- Beautiful

- Your motor is running great

- Magnifico

- You are on fire

- Wow! Look at you go

- You go girl

- Marvelous

- You're a super hero

- Outstanding

- Crowd pleaser

- You're flying high

- Whoo hoo

- You hit the bull's eye

- Now you got it

- Phenomenal

The frequency of reinforcement is another important consideration. The field of applied behavior analysis gives us a wealth of evidenced-based information. One such rule of thumb is that frequent reinforcement works well in the beginning and a variable rate of reinforcement is often more effective than a fixed rate of reinforcement (e.g. after every three tasks). This means that in the beginning, we need to make it easier to earn reinforcement, realizing that some children need to have reinforcement after every correct response to stay motivated, others can wait longer. Once motivation has shown improvement, we can then reinforce at irregular and increasingly longer intervals. We should strive to teach our children and students to wait for increasingly longer periods of time. To apply the variable rate of reinforcement rule of thumb, we would sometimes have our students complete a minimal amount of work to earn reinforcement, and at other times, more work. Remember, as stated earlier, our goal may simply be for the student to initiate and complete tasks. Later, we can emphasize accuracy in completing tasks in a certain time frame. Sometimes requiring a student to initiate and complete tasks accurately is too difficult in the beginning.

It is often possible to move a student along a continuum of being motivated extrinsically to one that is more intrinsic. Consider the following:

••

Aaron is a student with Asperger's syndrome who enjoyed reading and learning about anything related to the Pennsylvania turnpike. He knew all of the exits off the turnpike, where it was under construction, what the toll amounts were at various exits, and other features such as the order of the tunnels, major cities along the route, etc. Aaron had considerable difficulty in math and would often refuse to complete math work. His teacher developed a turnpike system of reinforcement whereby Aaron would earn a stamp on his turnpike card for completion of math that could be traded in for turnpike time later. During turnpike time, Aaron was free to explore the internet for turnpike-related activities. This extrinsic motivation system worked extremely well for Aaron. Today, Aaron wants to become better at math so that he "won't hold up the line at the toll booth" when he gets his job as an employee with the Pennsylvania Turnpike (intrinsic motivation). He is able to complete his math within specified time periods and at acceptable accuracy levels for his age.

As educators, we have to be open to the possibility that what motivates one student may not be what motivates others. As in the case of Aaron, he is motivated by something that is not typical of other children his age. Nevertheless, this is a powerful reinforcer for him. It is also a perseveration. Do not be afraid to utilize student perseverations as reinforcers. There is a wealth of research to support their effectiveness for some children. It will also help students to learn that there is a time and place for their perseverative interests.

★

Worksheet: Reinforcer Survey

1. What does the student like to play with or engage in?

   _____

2. In spare time at school, what does the student normally do?

   _____

3. What are the student's favorite foods?

   _____

4. What songs or music groups does the student like?

   _____

5. What are the student's favorite movies?

   _____

6. What are places that your student likes to go?

   _____

7. Who are the student's favorite adults in the school building?

   _____

8. Who are the student's favorite peers in the school building?

   _____

9. What classes or subjects does the student like best?

   _____

CHAPTER NINE

Self-Talk and Emotional Supports

In many contexts, stress is seen as a bad thing: a trigger that causes an individual to respond in a negative way. Stress comes about when demands are placed on our students, and there are many types of demands (social, academic, creative, athletic, etc.). But not all demands placed on students are "bad." A certain level of stress is needed to maintain attention, provide energy, and/or motivation. The way the student perceives the demand is what makes it a bad thing, and this is what has the capacity to increase his stress level.

We know that when someone is stressed, the levels of stress hormones are higher. The body is in a "fight" or "flight" mode of operation. The morning hours are when we all experience more demands on our bodies. We are awakening, dressing for work, preparing meals, completing last-minute chores as we strive to leave the house at an appropriate time so that we are not late for work. We may encounter traffic problems, drivers exhibiting unsafe behaviors as they, too, attempt to deal with their stress, animals jumping out into the road…all of these contribute to additional demands that may increase our stress hormones (cortisol, epinephrine, and norepinephrine). These hormonal changes may also cause us to engage in certain behaviors: social withdrawal, fidgeting, an increase in repetitive or compulsive behaviors, sleep disturbances, meal refusals, etc. It has been shown that many individuals with autism have an increased stress level as compared to their nonautistic peers (Tani *et al.* 2005). Some individuals will show higher levels of stress hormones upon exposure to certain demands (e.g. during the ride to school on the bus, engaging in physical education class, eating in a loud cafeteria, etc.).

It is not possible to eliminate all stress in a student's school day. However, we can certainly become more aware of a student's stressors, and in doing so, work to minimize them. But, more importantly, we need to teach our students to have self-awareness and to utilize coping strategies so that they can handle the demands of the school day appropriately.

Let's begin with minimizing stress:

- As discussed earlier, novel situations and new materials (worksheets, tests, textbooks, software) can bring on stress reactions for our students. Exposing the student to these in small doses repeatedly before requiring full participation or use is helpful in reducing stress. As an example, when a student moves to middle school and must transition to a variety of classes, providing him with a copy of his schedule and allowing him to rehearse finding the classrooms is extremely helpful. If fire alarms or noisy cafeterias are the problem, create interventions that provide minimal exposure, weaning the student into such situations slowly and with reinforcement for success.

- Make sure all materials are appropriately adapted.

- Utilize objective data collection to provide insight into what particular scenarios or experiences bring on stress for the student and then make appropriate accommodations or adaptations after the findings have been identified.

- Utilize student subjective data collection methods to help identify particular stressors (see the "Stress Detective Worksheet" on page 103).

- Utilize visual supports to show the student the routine of the day and when there are changes to the routine.

- Provide sensory rooms or areas of relaxation for the student to re-group.

- Identify a "safe" staff person—someone who has been pre-selected to process with the student any difficult, stressful scenarios.

- Problem-solve ways to reduce stressors—can physical education classes be adapted so that embarrassment does not have to occur? Can bullying and teasing be addressed proactively? How can we eliminate the stressors of the bus ride?

- Provide regular aerobic exercise in the school day—exercise has been shown to reduce stress. It can be a proactive way of overcoming anxiety.

Now let's discuss ways to teach the student how to handle his stress. Without effective means of dealing with stress, many students will succumb to the unhealthy by-products of too many stress hormones. He will engage in flight or fight behaviors. In schools today, we often create ways to help students *avoid* stress. However, for long-term success, avoiding stress is not always productive. As discussed earlier, experiencing some forms of stress is useful to help us make progress in our lives and in our personal relationships as well as our in our work environments. We will not always be able to avoid stress, especially stress that arises from unexpected events (e.g. experiencing loss, witnessing or experiencing trauma), but having good coping mechanisms will help us to survive these experience and be a precursor to good mental health.

Strategies to improve a student's ability to cope with stress include:

- Provide students with opportunities to brainstorm with trusted staff on what particular activities or events cause stress for students. The first step in dealing with stress is being aware of it (see the "Stress Detective Worksheet" on page 103).

- Students with limited ability to handle stress often lack "self-talk." Self-talk is the internal dialogue we often use to keep ourselves regulated. When confronted with stress, many of us do not yell, scream, hit, or punch. We utilize, albeit subconsciously, internal talk to regulate our emotions. Teaching the student particular phrases such as: "I can plow through it!", "This too shall pass", "I think I can, I think I can", "I can handle it because I'm just like a gum band; I'm flexible" can be extremely helpful. Pairing them with visuals in direct instruction will provide multi-sensory experiences that will make the learning more meaningful (see the box "I Can Plow Through My Work" on page 98).

- Teach the student what his body language says when stress begins to rise. Equate each level of body language to a particular level of stress. More importantly, attach to this level a particular activity the student can engage in to relieve the stress (see the box "Lava Levels of My Volcano" on page 100).

- Provide ways the student can learn to self-advocate in the form of phrases or activities that he can employ when he needs help or a break (break cards, help cards, safe passes, etc.).

- Teach relaxation strategies (yoga, self-meditation, exercise, using music) and practice these in calm moments, and cue to their use in stressful moments.

I Can Plow Through My Work: A Social Tale

When I am in school, sometimes I get upset.

If I can't do the work, or it's too hard, I sometimes want to give up.

Sometimes I start to complain. I say, "I HATE THIS!"

Sometimes I tell Mrs._____ that I'm not going to do the work.

I get really mad at myself and call myself stupid, especially when I make mistakes.

This is silly. Everyone makes mistakes! That's why pencils have erasers!

I know that I am not stupid. There are plenty of things that I do really well!

These things are _____, _____, and _____.

Everyone must practice things to get better!

When I am upset, I will pretend I am a snow plow. Snow plows scoop the snow up and move it aside. Snow plows make way for the next thing.

I can scoop my work up, complete it, and make way for the next thing too.

I can say, "I am plowing through!" Or, "It's O.K. to make mistakes, that's why pencils have erasers!"

Staff will need to remember that for most students, the above will not come easy. Merely showing the child a technique to use and then hoping he will put it into practice will most likely not be effective. Prompting the students to use the strategies and rehearsing them in calm moments will be necessary. Often implementation by the student will be slow and less effective at first.

Lastly, it is helpful to understand that for some children, stress levels appear to go from zero to ten fairly quickly. We should realize that for these children, the level of their stress is not immediately evident to us (and maybe to them!). They are most likely at a heightened level, and we have not noticed it. Perhaps their affect is not reflective of their internal states, or they have become fairly adept at hiding it as they attempt to avoid their outbursts. Most often, stress is rising throughout the day until one incident causes their "melt-down." Teaching these students to identify their stress levels during various parts of the day with a stress meter can be useful (see Figure 9.1 on page 101). This is a way for educators to touch base with the student, see how he is doing, and then coach him to put into place particular learned strategies if stress levels are on the rise. It will also empower him to realize that he can control his emotions.

Lava Levels of My Volcano

Level I	Lava Flowing	Take a Deep Breath
		Squeeze My Stress Toy
		Say to Myself: "I Can Stay Calm!"
Level II	Lava Rising	Use a Break Card for Five Minutes
		Put My Head Down to Cool Off
Level III	Lava Exploding	Ask to Leave
		No Hitting, Shouting, Throwing
		Take a Walk/ Get a Drink
		Go to Sensory Room

1	2	3
Low	Medium	High

Figure 9.1 Stress meter

When emotional disturbance is present in the school, administrators will need to decide if the environments they are creating are supportive. Supportive environments attempt to understand the meaning of melt-down behaviors, they are flexible in allowing the student to decompress, they are proactive in developing strategies to teach replacement skills, and they are team-oriented: they exhibit a willingness to work with families and outside professionals. On the opposite side are environments that are not supportive. Such environments are consequential or reactive to student stress, they are inflexible and unwilling to bend rules, they are perceived by families as unhelpful, unapproachable, or even uncompassionate.

The following is a checklist for administrators who are interested in creating a supportive environment for students who are experiencing stress or trauma:

- Is there a professional dedicated to being the "go-to" person for children experiencing stress in my building?

- Do we have a relaxation spot where students can go to re-group?

- Have staff received training on ways to teach stress management to their students?

- Does our school have a relationship with outside professionals who can serve as resources for our students and families, and do we encourage mutual communication between the school and these entities or professionals?

- Are we supportive of families and flexible with students we know are struggling? If not, how can we improve?

- Is there tangible evidence in our buildings that we are attempting to teach stress management strategies to our students?

The above can often be a helpful framework for administrators to begin thinking about ways to help students learn effective stress management. After all, academic grades are not the only indication of a student's ability to succeed. He must also be able to cope effectively with a variety of demands in his life.

★

Worksheet: Stress Detective

1. What assignments in the school day cause me to get stressed?

   _____

2. Are there certain people (kids or teachers) that cause me to get stressed?

   _____

   Why?

   _____

3. Are there certain subjects or classes that give me more stress than others?

   _____

   Why is that?

   _____

4. Am I more stressed in the morning or the afternoon?

   _____

5. Is there anything at home that may cause me stress? If so, what?

   _____

★

6. What activities in school cause me to be stressed (cafeteria, bus ride, etc.)?

   _____

7. Do I have difficultly sleeping or eating when I am stressed?

   _____

8. What activities help me to relax?

   _____

CHAPTER TEN

Attention

The number of preschool children being treated with medication for ADHD tripled between 1990 and 1995. The number of children ages 15 to 19 taking medication for ADHD has increased by 311 percent over 15 years. The use of medication to treat children between the ages of 5 and 14 also increased by approximately 170 percent. About 80 percent of the 11 million prescriptions written for methylphenidate (Ritalin is the brand name) each year are written for children. (Dunne 2008)

The Centers for Disease Control and Prevention states: "The prevalence of children aged 4–17 years of age taking ADHD medication increased from 4.8% in 2007 to 6.1% in 2011" (CDC 2013). Loe and Feldman (2007) state that pharmacologic treatment and behavior management are associated with reduction of the core symptoms of ADHD and increased academic productivity, but not with improved standardized test scores or ultimate educational attainment.

There are many side-effects that may occur as a result of the use of ADHD drugs. They include appetite suppression, weight loss, insomnia, nervousness, increase in blood pressure and heart rate, mood swings, anxiety, tics. As with any drug, it is important to weigh the benefits of medication with the goals for treatment. In schools today, educators often recommend ADHD drugs for children who have difficulty paying attention. However, I would suggest that there are other considerations that should be investigated first, and a host of strategies tried prior to taking the steps to medicate. Given the research that ADHD drugs may not increase learning as measured by standardized test scores, the decision to use pharmaceuticals to improve attention may not even be an option.

According to Dr. Mel Levin, we have several "systems" of attentional control, and understanding these is vital to implementing appropriate interventions. A good reference is the Misunderstood Minds website at www.pbs.org/wgbh/misunderstoodminds/attentiondiffs.html. Keep in mind that some children may have difficulty with one or more systems.

1. The first system is *mental energy*. Alertness, sleep and arousal balance, mental effort, and performance consistency fall into this area. Children with performance consistency problems show varying rates of being able to complete work. Some staff will say that a particular student appears to be tired on most days. But, often this child's performance is inconsistent across various days, or across parts of days. Some children will appear *very* tired at times, putting their heads down and falling asleep. Other students become tired half way through tasks. They may say, "I can't do it! I'm tired!" For this reason, we often link their performance to motivation, when, in actuality, it is mental energy. The cognitive process of being able to pay attention begins in the brain stem. Too much arousal makes us unable to concentrate, but too little

arousal can have the same effect. Medication is useful to aide in this process, but often is not enough. According to the National Institute for Mental Health's (NIMH) Multimodal Treatment Study of Children with ADHD completed in 1992, a combination of medication and behavior modification may be necessary to achieve optimal results.

2. The second system is *processing*. It contains a saliency determination (where the student must decide if the information is relevant and be inattentive to information that is not), depth and detail (this allows the student to adjust his/her attentiveness to focus on important details), cognitive activation (connecting prior knowledge learned to present situations), focal maintenance (making sure one can match the concentration required to the task at hand). Some tasks require more concentration than others (e.g. taking a shower vs. completing a science project). Last in this category is satisfaction control. This is the ability to match attention levels for low and preferred interest tasks. For example, consider a student who can pay attention to his video game for hours, but can't stay focused enough to do the social studies paper.

3. The third system is *production* and this involves the student's ability to preview, pace, self-monitor, inhibit (such as the ability to stop negative interferences or competing forces driving attention elsewhere) and hindsight (applying previous experiences and knowledge to get the job done).

Dr. Levin's research is only one theory as to how we "pay attention," and new research is becoming available daily. Michael Posner and Stephen Boies (1971) indicate that attention has three components: attention to sensory events, detecting signals for maintaining focus, and keeping alert or vigilant. Nevil Moray (1970) suggested there were six different meanings to the word "attention," and David Broadbent (1954) referred to attention as channels and suggested that we select which channels to "tune" into. More recent studies in 2014 from the Radiological Society of North America involved the use of MRI's. The results of these MRI tests have indicated that in children and adolescents diagnosed with ADHD, there are disrupted connections in the frontal lobes of the brain which cause difficulty with inhibitory control and strategic planning.

As educators, and with all this insightful knowledge, we have to drive our interventions to match the particular problems our kids have. The following is a list of "rule-outs" for kids who have difficulty paying attention:

1. Does the child have language impairment or difficulty understanding and processing language? If so, it would be important to supplement spoken language with other forms of communication (written, visuals, technology, etc.). A language evaluation, including auditory processing, may be useful in discovering underlying language deficits. Children with autism spectrum disorder clearly fall into this category as language impairment is one of the diagnostic criteria.

2. Does the child have sensory disturbances? Is he/she frequently distracted by noise, increased visual and auditory input, or movement? Would a smaller classroom or quieter work area/environment work better? Many classrooms today have so much sensory input that important directions are lost in a sea of stimuli. Creating a sensory-friendly classroom

can help to improve attention and focus. At the very least, creating a sensory-friendly spot for a student with preferential seating, free from distractions, can be helpful. Tucking distractions away with curtains or dividers can also be useful (see Figure 10.1). Many students are able to concentrate on important work when they are provided with a study carrel (see Figure 10.2). These interventions may help students who struggle with the second and third types of attention systems discussed earlier in this chapter.

Figure 10.1

Figure 10.2

3. As stated in previous chapters, some children need movement to be able to pay attention. Providing fidget toys or banded seat rungs (see Figures 10.3 and 10.4) can be a useful way to provide movement at the desk. So that a student's desk does not become a jungle of sensory gadgets, it's important to back each item, one at a time, with data collection to gauge its effectiveness. Students with arousal difficulties may be helped by these interventions. These types of interventions may also help students who have attentional issues in the first and second systems above.

Figure 10.3

Figure 10.4

4. Reinforcer systems, such as those discussed in Chapter 8, may help students demonstrating problems in system one as well.

5. The TWINK process (see Chapter 8) and graphic organizers may help students with attentional problems described in system two above.

6. Does the child do better when instruction is presented in multi-sensory formats so that he/she does not have to rely on one particular modality? We know that the least amount of learners learn best with auditory input. Unfortunately, much of our teaching in today's schools is done this way! If the preferred method of instruction is visual, then most of our teaching should be done this way. This may help reduce problems that are found in system one, since it's easier to pay attention to work that is geared for our preferred learning style or learning preferences, and there is less that we need to inhibit (system three) when we are engaged.

7. Is the amount of time the child is required to sit reasonable for his age? Today, children in school are asked to sit for longer and longer periods of time. Research tells us, however, that the optimal amount of time a child can sit is one minute per year of their age. Children who have opportunities for movement breaks (i.e. recess, exercise, etc.) often have better sustained attention ability. Thus, building in movement breaks *away from the desk and classroom* may improve sustained attention, especially for children who struggle with attention issues in system one.

8. In a study by Bar-David, Urkin, and Kozminsky (2005), students who were well-fed and well-hydrated were found to have better attention and score higher on cognitive assessments. Obviously, these two critical features can impact all of the three systems of attention.

9. Research by Kara Hume and Samuel Odom (2007) supports the use of timers and structured teaching, as well as the use of individual work station systems such as those advocated by TEACCH (the Training and Education of Autistic and Related Communication Handicapped Children), to promote the independent functioning of students with autism. Many children with disabilities, not necessarily those with autism spectrum disorder, benefit from structured teaching, task bins, when activities are laid out in a certain manner (left to right), and when hands-on work is presented in a concrete way. Task bins can be very helpful for those children who learn best by "doing" (see Figures 10.5 and 10.6). Structured teaching and multi-sensory activities benefit children who have difficulty with system three, but also can benefit those with systems one and two difficulties (see Figures 10.7 and 10.8).

10. Use technology! Children of this century are exposed to technology in increasingly larger numbers through iPads, iPhones, and computers. There are many educational applications that can assist children in the developmental of social, emotional, academic skills, as well as life skills. Often technology appeals to students because it is fast-paced, engaging (music, lights, etc.), and

hands-on. Educators frequently note that children who are taught using a Smart Board or Interactive Whiteboard show more engagement and higher rates of retention (Thompson and Thompson 2005). The use of technology in the classroom is on the rise and there is lots of research to support its effectiveness. Hopefully, with this increased prevalence of technology in our schools will come additional opportunities for students who struggle to find success in the classroom, especially for learners with disabilities.

Figure 10.5

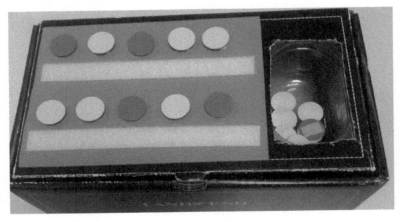

Figure 10.6

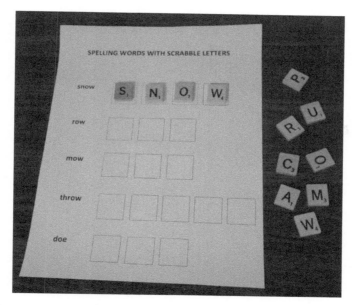

Figure 10.7 Use of Scrabble tiles (a tactile activity) to teach spelling

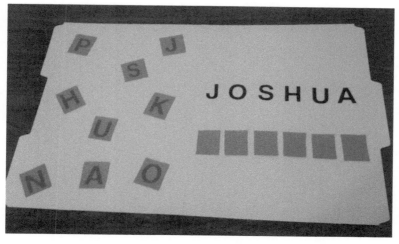

Figure 10.8 Use of velcro letters (a tactile
activity) to teach name recognition

Conclusion

Many educators who have been in the classroom for a long period of time will say that they have never seen so many students with disabilities and learning problems in their classrooms as they do today. They have been forced to learn entirely different ways to teach in order to meet the increased performance demands placed upon them by their school districts and state and federal governments. What once was a relatively restriction-free teaching environment where creativity and teacher-choice governed the pace and practices in the classroom, is now an environment where progress is monitored continually, and teaching methodologies are refined and shaped.

Despite all of the regulatory mandates, policies and procedures, there lies one basic reason why educators and parents should be interested in reaching and teaching children with executive function deficits, and it is a moral one. Children with these difficulties *deserve it*. Their very future *depends on it*.

> "If they can't learn the way we teach, maybe
> we should teach the way they learn."
>
> *author unknown*

References

Baddeley, A. (1996) 'Exploring the central executive.' *Quarterly Journal of Experimental Psychology: Human Experimental Psychology 49a,* 5–28.

Bar-David, Y., Urkin, J., and Kozminsky, E. (2005) 'The effect of voluntary dehydration on cognitive functions of elementary schoolchildren.' *Acta Paediatrica 94,* 11, 1667–1673.

Barkley, R. (1997) 'Behavioral inhibition, sustained attention, and executive functions: Constructing a unifying theory of ADHD.' *Psychological Bulletin 121,* 1, 65–94.

Bianchi L. (1922) *The Mechanisms of the Brain and the Function of the Frontal Lobes* (J. H. MacDonald, Trans.) Edinburgh: E. & S. Livingstone.

Bronowski, J. (1977) *A Sense of the Future.* Cambridge, MA: MIT Press.

Broadbent, D.E. (1954) 'The role of localization in attention and memory span.' *Journal of Experimental Psychology 47,* 191–196.

Casey, B.J., Sommerville, L.H., Gotlib, I.H., Ayduk, O. *et al.* (2011) 'Behavioral and neural correlates of delay of gratification 40 years later.' *Proceedings of the National Academy of Sciences 108,* 36, 14998–15003.

Centers for Disease Control and Prevention (2011) 'Attention-Deficit/ Hyperactivity Disorder (ADHD): Data and Statistics' [Online article]. Available at www.cdc.gov/ncbddd/adhd/data.html, acessed 4 June 2014.

Cooper, J., Heron, T., and Heward, W. (2007) *Applied Behavioral Analysis.* New York, NY: Pearson.

Corcoran, R., Cahill, C., and Frith, C.D. (1997) 'The appreciation of visual jokes in people with schizophrenia: A study of mentalizing ability.' *Schizophrenia Resource 24,* 319–327.

Crooke, P., Hendrix, R., and Rachman, J. (2008) 'Measuring the effectiveness of teaching social thinking to children with autism spectrum disorder.' *Journal of Autism and Developmental Disorders 38*, 3, 581–591.

Dettmer, S., Simpson R.L., Myles B, and Granz, J.B. (2000) 'The use of visual supports to facilitate transitions of students with autism.' *Focus on Autism and Other Disabilities 15*, 163–170.

Dunne, D.W. (2008) 'Statistics Confirm Rise in Childhood ADHD and Medication Use' [Online article]. Available at www.educationworld.com/a_issues/issues148a.shtml, accessed on 13 June 2014.

Fuster, J. (1989) 'Memory and Planning: Two Temporal Perspectives of Frontal Lobe Function.' In H.S. Jasper, S. Riggio, and P.S. Goldman-Rakic (eds) *Epilepsy and the Functional Anatomy of the Frontal Lobe.* New York, NY: Raven Press.

Goldberg, E. (2001) *The Executive Brain: Frontal Lobes and the Civilized Mind.* New York, NY: Oxford University Press.

Golden, C., Freshwater, S., and Golden, Z. (2002) *The Stroop Color and Word Test.* Wood Dale, IL: Stoelting.

Grant, D. and Berg, E. (2003) *The Wisconsin Card Sorting Test, WCST.* Lutz, FL: PAR, Inc.

Happé, F.G.E. (1994) 'An advanced theory of mind: Understanding of story characters' thoughts and feelings by able autistic, mentally handicapped, and normal children and adults.' *Journal of Autism and Developmental Disorders 24*, 129–154.

Holmes, J.M. (1987) 'Natural Histories in Learning Disabilities, Neuropsychological Difference/Environmental Demand.' In S.J. Ceci (ed.) *Handbook of Cognitive, Social, and Neuropsychological Aspects of Learning Disabilities: Volume 2.* Hillsdale, NJ: Lawrence Erlbaum.

Hume, K. and Odom, S. (2007) 'Effects of an Individual Work System on the independent functioning of students wth autism.' *Journal of Autism and Developmental Disorders 37*, 6, 1166–1180.

Loe, I.E. and Feldman, H.M. (2007) 'Academic and educational outcomes of children with ADHD.' *Journal of Pediatric Psychology 32*, 643–654.

Miller, G. (1956) 'The magical number seven, plus or minus two: Some limits on our capacity for processing information.' *Psychological Review 63*, 2, 81–97.

Moray, N. (1970) 'Towards a quantitative theory of attention.' *Acta Psychologica 33*, 111–117.

Moyes, R. (2002) *Addressing the Challenging Behavior of Children with High-Functioning Autism/Asperger's Syndrome in the Classroom.* London: Jessica Kingsley Publishers.

Paivio, A. (1971) *Imagery and Verbal Processes*. New York, NY: Holt, Rinehart, and Winston.

Pennington, B.F. and Oszonoff, S. (1996) 'Executive functions and developmental psychopathology.' *Journal of Child Psychology and Psychiatry 37*, 1, 51–87.

Piaget, J. (1954) *The Construction of Reality in a Child* (M. Cook, Trans.). New York, NY: Basic Books.

Posner, M. and Boies, S. (1971) 'Components of attention.' *Psychological Review 78*, 5, 391–408.

Tani, P., Lindberg, M., Matto, V., Appelberg, B., Nieminen-von Wendt, T., von Wendt, L., *et al.* (2005) 'High plasma HCTS levels in adults with Asperger's syndrome.' *Journal of Psychosomatic Research 58*, 6, 533–536.

Thompson, M. and Thompson, J. (2005) *Learning-Focused Strategies Notebook*. Boone, NC: Learning Concepts.

Wimmer, H. and Perner, J. (1983) 'Beliefs about beliefs: Representation and constraining function of wrong beliefs in young children's understanding of deception.' *Cognition 13*, 1, 103–128.

Index

special education classes
  and executive function
      deficits 19–22
stress
  description of 94–5
  interventions for 95–102
  worksheet for 103–4
Stroop Test 53–4

Tani, P. 95
technology
  as attention intervention 113–4
theory of mind
  assessment of 59–61
  and autism spectrum
      disorders 57–9
  and executive function
      deficits 22–3
  lesson plan for 62–3
  and social skills 58
Thompson, J. 114
Thompson, M. 114
time management
  as domain of executive
      functions 23
Tourette's syndrome
  and behavioral inhibition 27–8
Training and Education of Autistic
    and Related Communication
    Handicapped Children
    (TEACCH) 113
transitions
  for behavioral inhibition 47–51
  ideas for 47–51

Urkin, J. 113

Wimmer, H. 59
Wisconsin Card Sorting Test 54
working memory

as domain of executive
      functions 22–3
hierarchy of 65–6
importance of 64
interventions for 68–9
use in schools 66–9
worksheets
  for behavioral inhibition 36–7
  for project planning and
      organization 81–2
  for reinforcers 93
  for stress 103–4